Fort Scott

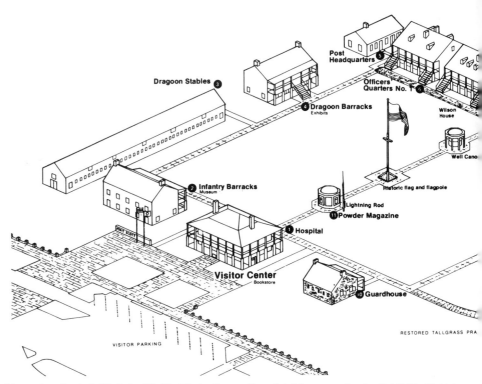

Follow this map for a close look at the fort and the life of the frontier army. The main buildings are numbered and briefly identified below.

❶ Built in 1843 for the treatment of the sick and wounded, now used as the fort's visitor center. One of the two original wards is refurnished. *Restoration*

❷ The original barracks on this site was constructed in 1844, some work being done by units of the 4th Infantry. The present building houses a museum. *Reconstruction*

❸ The original stables (built 1843) held over 80 stalls for horses and several rooms for storing feed and tack. Prairie hay was purchased locally and stored loose (not baled) in the loft. *Reconstruction.*

❹ First occupied by Co A of the 1st Draoons in 1844. The soldiers bunked on the upper level, took their meals in the mess hall on the ground floor. *Reconstruction*

❺ The commanding officer and his adjutant ran the post from this building. It held their offices, a court-marial room, and storerooms for artillery. *Reconstruction*

❻ Officers and their families lived comfortably in houses like this. Captain Swords and his wife occupied one unit of this duplex. *Restoration*

Fort Scott
National Historic Site

Carriage House

Outbuilding

Outbuilding

RESTORED TALLGRASS PRAIRIE

Carriage House

Site of Blair House

Officers' Quarters
No 4

Quartermaster
Storehouse

Post Bakery

Infantry
Barracks
Restrooms

Cistern

Blacksmith
Shop

Quartermaster Quadrangle

Privy Foundations

The Quartermaster Quad-
rangle contained grain
bins, corn cribs, an ice
house, a stable for
draft stock, and shops
for carpenters, black-
smiths, and saddlers.

Tallgrass prairie once
covered eastern Kansas
This is one of two areas
at Fort Scott being re-
stored to natural prairie

RESTORED TALLGRASS PRAIRIE

BUS AND RV PARKING

Service Road

7 The post's diverse military supplies —everything needed to put a fighting force into the field —were delivered to, stored in, and issued from this building. *Restoration*

8 Bread was a staple of the soldier's diet. His daily ration (18 ounces) was baked in ovens here by bakers chosen from each company on a rotating basis. *Restoration*

9 This shop is the only original structure remaining from the Quartermaster Quadrangle. Here tools were made and sharpened, equipment was repaired and horses, mules and oxen were shod. *Restoration*

10 Military discipline was strict in the frontier army. Solitary confinement and a diet of bread and water were common punishments for enlisted men. *Reconstruction*

11 The magazine, completed in 1844 and demolished in 1868, gave safe storage to the fort's explosives: powder, cartridges, fuses, and primers. *Reconstruction*

Fort Scott National Historic Site is administered by the National Park Service, U.S. Department of the Interior.

A superintendent, whose address is Old Fort Boulevard, Fort Scott, Kansas 66701, is in immediate charge.

Fort Scott was named to honor General-in-Chief of the Army Winfield Scott (1786–1866). A native of Virginia, Scott was commissioned a captain of light artillery in 1808 and saw duty during the War of 1812. He was appointed brigadier general in 1814 and shortly thereafter was brevetted a major general. He studied military tactics after the war, and he was a prime mover in the cause of temperance in the army. He served in the Black Hawk War, 1832; led troops during the Seminole War in Florida, 1835; and helped restore peace along the Canadian border in 1838. He oversaw the removal of the Cherokees to present Oklahoma. In June 1841 he was named general-in-chief of the army. Although the small post west of the Missouri border was named to honor Scott, the general was not pleased to have a small, obscure, frontier fort bear his name. He said that the action had been taken by Secretary of War John C. Spencer "without my knowledge and against my wishes." Scott worked hard to increase professionalism in the army, helped eradicate extremely harsh disciplinary actions and cruel punishments, and urged better education of the officer class. He was called "Fuss and Feathers" because of his adherence to proper dress and decorum. Scott oversaw the military campaign against Mexico, 1846–1848, and personally commanded the invasion force from Vera Cruz to Mexico City that led to the defeat of Mexico. In 1852 he was the Whig candidate for president but was defeated by Franklin Pierce. He warned of the coming Civil War in 1860, and he directed the protection of the nation's capital when the war came. Although a Virginian, Scott was loyal to the Union. He retired November 1, 1861, at age seventy-five. He died at West Point a few days before his eightieth birthday and was buried in the national cemetery at the military academy. Painting by Minor K. Kellogg, 1851.

Fort Scott

Courage and Conflict on the Border

by Leo E. Oliva

Kansas State Historical Society
Topeka, Kansas

THE AUTHOR: Dr. Leo E. Oliva is a former university professor of history. He farms with his wife, Bonita, in Rooks County, Kansas, and is the owner of Western Book publishing company. In addition Oliva is a free-lance historian whose writing and research has focused on the frontier army and Indians as well as local history. This booklet was originally published in 1984 as part of a series Oliva prepared on Kansas forts for the Kansas State Historical Society. His *Fort Hays, Frontier Army Post, 1865-1889* was released in 1980, and *Fort Larned on the Santa Fe Trail* was printed in 1982. Oliva's other publications include *Soldiers on the Santa Fe Trail* (1967), *Ash Rock and the Stone Church: The History of a Kansas Rural Community* (1983), and *Fort Union and the Frontier Army in the Southwest* (1993). Leo and Bonita Oliva are both former sheriffs of the Kansas Corral of the Westerners.

FRONT COVER: *Watching Parade*, Fort Scott, Kansas, 1842–1853, by Jerry D. Thomas. Thomas, a nationally acclaimed artist, has made a career of creating wildlife and western art. His original works will appear on the covers of all eight volumes of the Kansas Forts Series. Thomas is a resident of Manhattan, Kansas.

Fort Scott: Courage and Conflict on the Border is the first volume in the Kansas Forts Series published by the Kansas State Historical Society in cooperation with the Kansas Forts Network.

Original title: Fort Scott on the Indian Frontier
Copyright© 1984 Kansas State Historical Society
Second printing 1990
Revised edition 1996

Library of Congress Card Catalog Number 84-081183
ISBN 0-87726-027-3

Printed by H.M. Ives & Sons, Inc., Topeka, Kansas

Contents

FOREWORD

Fort Scott: Courage and Conflict on the Border is a brief history of Fort Scott, Kansas, from 1842 to 1873. During this period in American history the town of Fort Scott evolved from a small military fort, established to assist with the protection and maintenance of the permanent Indian Frontier, into a large railroad boomtown of the 1870s. The town was socially and politically divided by the sectional and regional conflict that preceded the American Civil War. During the war it was occupied continually by Union forces, became a large supply depot and refugee haven, and was critical to the defense of eastern Kansas and the Midwest. Fort Scott is the only major town still existing in Kansas that developed from a U.S. Army fort established before Kansas became a territory and a state.

Today Fort Scott National Historic Site is part of the National Park System, and its significance is identified in its enabling legislation that states it will "commemorate the role that Fort Scott played in the opening of the west, the Civil War and the strife that preceded the Civil War in the state of Kansas." Fort Scott has been designated as one of eight major forts in Kansas history; the remaining seven include Fort Leavenworth (1827–present), Fort Riley (1853–present), Fort Larned (1859–1878), Fort Harker (1864–1872), Fort Dodge (1865–1882), Fort Wallace (1865–1882), and Fort Hays (1865–1889). All of these forts participated in the westward expansion of the United States across the Central Plains and the settlement of Kansas. At various times each fort served as a military supply depot, assisted with the protection of travelers and settlers, and facilitated the construction of railroads across the Plains. Some of the Kansas forts periodically were charged with protecting the rights of specific Native American tribes. The forts distributed annuities guaranteed by treaty agreements and were the location of Indian agencies.

Fort Scott: Courage and Conflict on the Border is the first in a series of books about each of the eight historic forts in Kansas. The Kansas Forts Series is being published by the Kansas State Historical Society in cooperation with the National Park Service, U.S. Army Museums, Forts Leavenworth and Riley, and local historical societies to document and assist with the preservation of these momentous Kansas and national resources.

Arnold W. Schofield, historian
Fort Scott National Historic Site

1

The Founding of Fort Scott

ort Scott was established in 1842 on the Fort Leavenworth–Fort Gibson military road as part of a network of outposts designed to protect western settlers and Indians. The rapid westward expansion of the nation's pioneers and the removal of eastern Indian tribes to lands west of the Mississippi River had created a two-sided problem for the military; protection of settlers from Indians and protection of Indians from settlers and other tribes. It was hoped that a so-called "permanent Indian frontier," beyond which Indians could enjoy their traditional cultures free from white encroachment and behind which settlers could pursue their dreams without fear of retaliation, would prevent conflicts. For a few years it seemed as though it might work, provided the army at the frontier forts could enforce the separation. Unfortunately the expansionist pressures of the United States in the 1840s, called "Manifest Destiny" by some, destroyed that line of demarcation and touched off a lengthy struggle farther west. The active years of Fort Scott (1842–1853) spanned the era of transition.

The Indian Removal Act of 1830 established a policy under consideration for many years to remove tribes east of the Mississippi River to lands west of that river. During the next decade more than eighty thousand Indians were moved, mostly to lands west of Missouri and Arkansas in present Kansas and Oklahoma. In 1834 Congress passed new legislation to govern Indian–white relations, including regulation of trade, preservation of peace, strict control of contacts between whites and

1

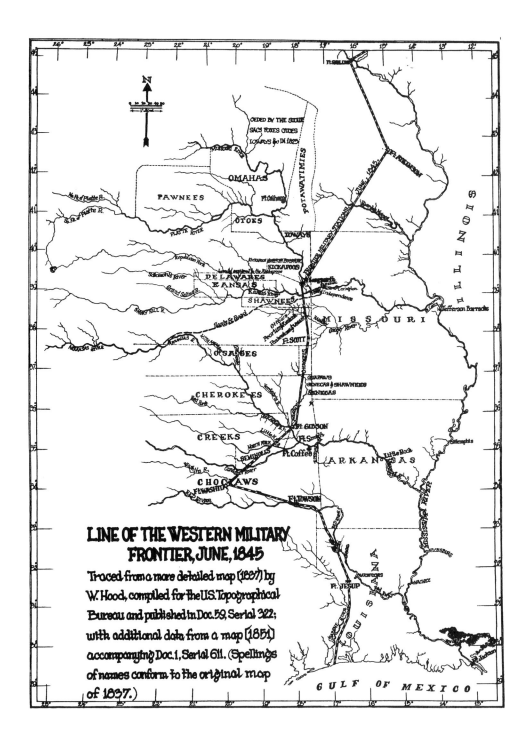

LINE OF THE WESTERN MILITARY FRONTIER, JUNE, 1845

Traced from a more detailed map (1837) by W. Hood, compiled for the U.S. Topographical Bureau and published in Doc. 59, Serial 322; with additional data from a map (1851) accompanying Doc. 1, Serial 611. (Spellings of names conform to the original map of 1837.)

Indians, and the use of the military to enforce the act. Fulfillment of the regulations required a new plan for frontier defense.

In 1836 Secretary of War Lewis Cass recommended a north-south line of forts along the western frontier, connected by a military road. His proposal was enacted the same year when President Andrew Jackson signed a law to provide better protection of the frontier. It provided for the survey and construction of a military road from the upper Mississippi River in the north to the Red River in the south, passing west of the states of Missouri and Arkansas, with the condition that permission be secured from the Indian tribes through whose lands the road passed. It also provided for the construction of military posts along the road — in addition to those already in the region — at sites to be selected later, authorized the use of troops to perform the labor, and appropriated one hundred thousand dollars to get the job done. Because of changes in administrations and the economic depression which began in 1837, the plan was not implemented immediately.

Earlier requests were submitted to Congress for a road south from Fort Leavenworth (established on the Missouri River in 1827). In 1835 a petition for a mail route from Fort Leavenworth to Fort Towson (established near the Red River in 1824) was presented to the House of Representatives. Signatories included dragoon officers stationed at Fort Leavenworth, citizens of western Missouri, and missionaries among the removed tribes. A similar request was made early in 1836. Colonel Henry Dodge, First Dragoons, commanding at Fort Leavenworth, recommended a military road from his post to Fort Gibson (established in 1824 approximately fifty miles west of the Arkansas state line on the left bank of the Neosho River about two and one-half miles from its confluence with the Arkansas River just east of present Muskogee, Oklahoma) to facilitate the movement of troops. A mail route was established during 1836, and the provisions of the Defense Act of 1836 later resulted in the construction of the requested military road on which Fort Scott was established.

There was, however, some delay while the best methods of dealing with frontier defense were evaluated. The region of frontier conflicts was found mainly within a great arc of territory extending from west of the Great Lakes to the Gulf of Mexico, including much of present Minnesota, Iowa, Nebraska, Kansas, Oklahoma, Texas, and adjoining regions east and west. Although the federal army was small — only 7,834 men to guard the entire nation in 1837 — and Congress was unwilling to increase military expenditures during the depression that began the same year, consideration of plans to provide protection for settlers and Indians continued.

The proposal for a line of forts to guard the frontier was modified with the recommendation for two lines of forts. An exterior line of posts would be established in the Indian country, stretching from Fort Snelling (founded in 1819 at the confluence of the Minnesota and Mississippi Rivers) on the north, through Fort Leavenworth, to Fort Towson. Troops stationed along this exterior line could protect the Indians. An interior line farther east could protect the settlers and provide reinforcements to the exterior line as needed. This proposal considered roads connecting the interior posts to the exterior forts as being more important than the road connecting the exterior line. These recommendations had merit, but the cost was more than Congress would authorize. Besides, Congress already had provided for the frontier military road and wanted to know how it was progressing.

Conflicts between whites and Indians occurred all along the frontier, but the situation was particularly troublesome west of Missouri and Arkansas where the eastern tribes had been relocated. Troubles also existed between Indians from the East and the indigenous tribes in the West. The Osages were especially hostile toward the removed Cherokees and the settlers in western Missouri, territory which had once been claimed by the Osages. The Osages gave up claims to millions of acres for a specified reservation in 1825. In 1833 a small party of Indian commissioners, seeking a new treaty with the Osages, reported that the tribe comprised a population of about six thousand and that "the Osages are a poor, almost naked and half starved people."

Their poverty reportedly contributed to their raiding. Sometimes whiskey traders and other traders took advantage of them, and the behavior of white settlers sometimes provoked Osage retaliation. In 1837, for example, a band of Osages was caught in Missouri, and a local militia unit whipped the Indians and drove them from the state. Two companies of dragoons from Fort Leavenworth, led by Captain Edwin V. Sumner, arrived during that confrontation and helped pacify the situation. Osages returned to Missouri settlements in 1838, and people were killed on both sides. Troops were sent from Forts Leavenworth and Gibson. The troubles helped show that the frontier forts were spaced too far apart to keep order and prevent bloodshed. The arrival of many more eastern Indians during the late 1830s promised more trouble. The need for the military road and new forts seemed clear.

In the autumn of 1837 Charles Dimmock, surveyor, and his military escort (Colonel Stephen W. Kearny, Captain Nathan Boone, Lieutenants Philip Kearny and Philip R. Thompson, and Company H, First Dragoons)

4

Stephen Watts Kearny (1794–1848) helped with the survey of the Fort Leavenworth–Fort Gibson road in 1837. He led troops over that route in 1839. Kearny entered military service during the War of 1812, attaining the rank of captain; he remained in the army and rose to the rank of major, Third Infantry, in 1829. In 1833 he was appointed lieutenant colonel of the newly organized regiment of dragoons (later known as First Dragoons), and he was promoted to colonel in 1836. He led dragoons, including some from Fort Scott, on an expedition to the Rocky Mountains in 1845. Kearny was promoted to brigadier general and placed in command of the Army of the West in 1846. He led the invasion of Mexico via the Santa Fe Trail, took possession of New Mexico, established a provisional civil government at Santa Fe, marched on to California, and helped secure that province for the United States. He was brevetted a major general, 1846, and was military governor of California, 1847. He died in 1848 at St. Louis.

explored the area between Fort Leavenworth and the Arkansas River. Dimmock and his assistant, a Mr. Minor, surveyed a route from Fort Coffee (founded in 1834 on the right bank of the Arkansas River about twelve miles west of the present Arkansas boundary) to Fort Leavenworth between September 27 and November 8, 1837. The proposed road, later known as the Fort Leavenworth–Fort Gibson military road, ran just west

Western Frontier Military
ROAD.

THE undersigned having been directed to put under contract that portion of the Western Frontier Military Road extending from the Marais de Cygne, to Spring River, about

85 MILES,

invites all those who may be desirous of becoming Contractors for any portion of this work, and wish to become acquainted with the topography of the country through which the survey passes, to meet him at Westport, Mo., on **THURSDAY**, the 19th inst., & accompany him in an examination of the Route.

The whole distance will be divided into sections of convenient lengths, and each section offered for contract separately. **De**tailed plans of the different sections will be prepared as soon as the route shall have been examined, and due notice given of the time when the contracts will be let.

The following extract from the act of Congress, defines the mode of construction:

"The timber shall be cut down to a reasonable width, and the "wet and marshy places shall be causewayed or otherwise ren- "dered passable; cheap bridges shall be erected on the smaller "streams not having good fords across them; and when it may "be found necessary, the road may be thrown up in the centre."

THO'S. SWORDS, *Capt. A. Q. M.*

Asst. Qr. Master's Office,
Fort Leavenworth, Sept. 10, 1839.

of the western boundaries of Arkansas and Missouri; the total length was 286 miles. Kearny and Boone recommended that new forts be located along this route and suggested the crossings of the Spring and Marais des Cygnes Rivers as possible sites.

At the end of 1837 Secretary of War Joel Poinsett submitted to Congress his plan for frontier defense. It called for a line of forts from Fort Snelling to Fort Jesup (established in 1822 in western Louisiana), utiliz-

Ethan Allen Hitchcock (1798–1870), a Vermont native, was graduated from West Point in 1817, after which he taught there. He was investigating fraud and profiteering in the removal of eastern tribes when he visited the West in 1841–1842 and recommended the abandonment of Fort Wayne and the location of a new post that became Fort Scott. He later served in the Mexican War, first under General Zachary Taylor and then under General Winfield Scott. He resigned from the army in 1855 and lived in St. Louis. He served as a major general of volunteers during the Civil War. He died at St. Louis, August 5, 1870.

ing the established forts and proposing additional posts to fill the gaps. Other plans were submitted by military officers, which called for similar construction and an increase in the size of the army. Eventually a plan was effected by bits and pieces.

In 1838 work began on the road south from Fort Leavenworth to the Marais des Cygnes River, a distance of seventy-two miles. That portion was completed in 1839, and work began on the next section to Spring River, approximately eighty-six miles, which was completed in 1840. The final section to Fort Gibson apparently was not completed until the mid-1840s, if in fact it was completed at all, but the route was used by military and civilian traffic throughout the era.

In 1839 Colonel Kearny and five companies of First Dragoons traveled to Fort Wayne (founded the previous year) and back to Fort Leavenworth over the new route. In 1844 a party of missionaries traveled the road from Shawnee Methodist Mission to Indian Territory (present Oklahoma). Following damaging floods in the spring of 1844, which washed out many of the bridges, requests were made to repair it. Captain Thomas Swords wrote Quartermaster General Thomas Jesup, August 27, 1844:

This road is highly important as a military communication; and, being the only direct route from the northwestern part of Missouri and Iowa to Arkansas and Texas, it has been much travelled, and those accustomed to use it will be put to great inconvenience by its present condition. I recommend that the bridges be replaced, and the road repaired by the labor of troops as a sufficient force can be spared for the purpose.

Meanwhile, on the Arkansas River, Fort Smith was built into a major post. Fort Coffee, not far from Fort Smith, was abandoned (1838), and a new post was established approximately eighty miles north of Fort Smith on the Illinois River on Cherokee lands. The initial site proved unhealthy, and the fort was relocated on Spavinaw Creek, a tributary of the Neosho River, just west of the northwest corner of Arkansas, and named Fort Wayne. This new post, located in the midst of the Cherokees, could protect the Indians and keep an eye on them at the same time. Internal fighting among the various Cherokee factions was also a problem. A large number of troops assembled in the region, and the Cherokees agreed to stop fighting each other.

The Cherokees were not happy with the presence of Fort Wayne in their midst. In 1841 a Cherokee delegation in Washington asked the president to remove the post. General Zachary Taylor, commanding the military division, recommended abandonment of Fort Wayne. Major Ethan Allen Hitchcock, who was in the region investigating Indian affairs for the War Department, reported the Cherokee opposition and recommended its abandonment. Hitchcock stated there was no longer a need for troops among the Cherokees and summed up their opposition:

> The Cherokees have justly complained that a Military force has been unnecessarily established in one of the finest portions of their country — in the midst of an orderly industrious and sober community — bringing with it a train of evils before comparatively unknown — exposing their women to seduction and even to violence and inviting the location of dram shops immediately upon the State line opposite the post. (The intercourse Act and the Cherokee laws forbid the introduction of whiskey into the Nation.) At one of these shops only a few months ago, two Cherokees were murdered by some soldiers, whose trial and acquittal have in no manner removed the impression entertained by every body that the soldiers were the guilty party.

Hitchcock recommended that the garrison at Fort Wayne be moved farther north to establish a new post "in what has been called the neutral ground (now belonging to the Cherokees) between the Osage Indians and the State of Missouri — at some point about 100 miles south of Fort

Artist George Catlin vis-
ited many western Indian
tribes including the
Osages, wrote about their
cultures, and painted
portraits and scenes from
their lives. These paint-
ings show the dress and
ornamentation of several
leading Osages in the
1830s. Of this tribe,
Catlin wrote:

"The Osages may justly
be said to be the tallest
race of men in North
America, either of red or
white skins; there being
very few indeed of the
men, at their full growth,
who are less than six feet
in stature, and very many
of them six and a half,
and others seven feet. . . .

Their movement is graceful and quick; and in war and the chase, I think they
are equal to any of the tribes about them."

Of their condition in 1834, Catlin stated:

"The Osages have been formerly, and until quite recently, a powerful and
warlike tribe; carrying their arms fearlessly through all of these realms; and
ready to cope with foes of any kind that they were liable to meet. At present,
the case is quite different; they have been repeatedly moved and jostled along,
. . . and reduced by every war and every move. The small-pox has taken its
share of them at two or three different times; . . . so that their decline has
been very rapid, bringing them to the mere handful that now exists of them;
though still preserving their valour as warriors, which they are continually
shewing off as bravely and as professionally as they can, . . . although they
are the principal sufferers in those scenes which they fearlessly persist in, as
if they were actually bent on their self-destruction. Very great efforts have
been, and are being made amongst these people to civilize and christianize
them; and still I believe with but little success. Agriculture they have caught
but little of; and of religion and civilization still less."

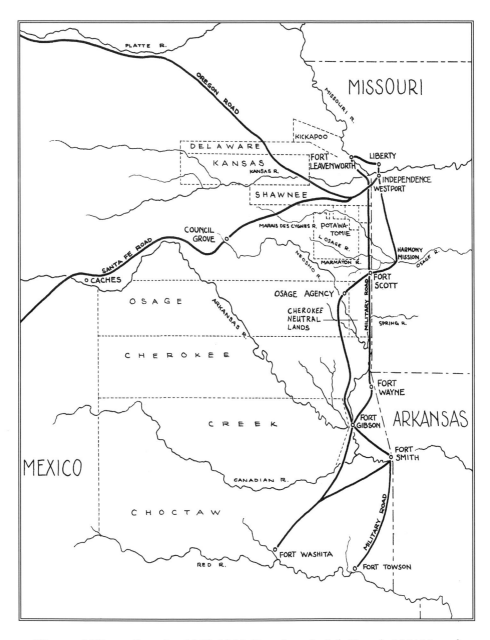

Western Military Frontier, 1842–1846. Based on Josiah Gregg's 1844 Map of the Indian Territory. *Map drawn by Michael C. Snell.*

John Hamilton (ca. 1816–1876) joined the dragoons in 1835. In 1842 he was a sergeant in that regiment, stationed at Fort Wayne. He accompanied the commission that selected the location for Fort Scott, and he directed the construction of temporary quarters there prior to the arrival of the garrison. As Hamilton later recalled, "I cut the 1st tree down myself that helpd [sic] build the 1st House that was ever built in Fort Scott." He served as quartermaster sergeant at Fort Scott until he was transferred to Fort Jesup, Louisiana. Hamilton was back at Fort Scott by 1853, and he purchased some of the military property auctioned there on April 16, 1855. Between 1855 and 1861 Hamilton was a free-state conservative living in Fort Scott and then near the Marmaton River. In June 1858 the territorial governor appointed him president of a local peace commission that developed a series of resolutions, known as the Denver peace treaty, to restore civil order in Fort Scott and Bourbon County. The peace treaty failed to stop the guerrilla warfare, and Hamilton was appointed a deputy sheriff of Bourbon County. He also was commissioned a captain, commanding one of the two local militia companies raised to help maintain peace and order in the county. His Civil War activities are not known, although he may have been in the state militia. About 1865 he settled in Crawford County, where he was elected to the state legislature. He died at Independence, Kansas, in 1876.

Leavenworth; perhaps near where the Military road crosses the Marmiton [Marmaton] would be a good site." Actually the Marmaton River was north of the Cherokee neutral ground on land set aside for the New York Indians, including members of the following tribes: Seneca, Onondaga, Cayuga, Tuscarora, Oneida, St. Regis, Stockbridge, Munsee, and Brothertown. Hitchcock's recommended location was based on his

Benjamin Davis Moore (1810–1846), Kentucky native, began military service as a midshipman in the U.S. Navy, 1829. He resigned in 1832 and was appointed a lieutenant of the Regiment of Mounted Rangers. In 1833 he transferred to the dragoons, where he was promoted to captain in 1837. Captain Moore helped choose the location of Fort Scott, and he was the first post commander. Moore and his Company C were transferred to Fort Leavenworth in 1843, from which post he saw service on the Santa Fe Trail. When the war with Mexico began in 1846, Moore became part of Kearny's Army of the West. He marched to California, where he was killed at the Battle of San Pasqual, December 6, 1846.

assessment of the Osages, whom he had described on an earlier occasion: "The Osage tribe is out of favor with all their neighbors. They are thieves to a man, wild, ignorant and barbarous, hate work and are half the time in a starving condition." In his letter of January 9, 1842, recommending the establishment of a new post, Hitchcock stated:

> West of the Neutral ground are the Osages, the greatest thieves near the frontier and who have committed more depredations in Missouri than all the other Indians together along the whole line of the two States of Arkansas and Missouri. These are the Indians, and not the Cherokees that require to be over-awed by the presence of a Military force. North of the Osages are the Pottawotomies who are rather a dissatisfied people and are more likely to enter into a hostile combination than any other Indians.

> A post on the neutral ground would be at all times ready to chastise Osage marauders and by thus protecting the people of Missouri prevent a border difficulty which has several times been on the point of breaking out. An undisciplined militia has repeatedly been on the point of carry-

ing blood shed among the Osages for thefts committed by them when rendered almost desperate by starvation.

A post on the neutral ground would also be in a favorable position to act in concert if necessary, with troops from Ft. Leavenworth upon the Pottawotomies without exciting them by being permanently among them. Such a post could be supplied or supply itself as readily as this of Fort Wayne.

Colonel George Croghan, inspector general of western forts from 1825 to 1845, recommended in 1827 the establishment of a military post on the Neosho River to keep watch over the Osages. He suggested that mounted troops would be required to deal effectively with Plains tribes. He made a similar recommendation in 1833, pointing out that the newly organized dragoons would be ideal troops to garrison the post.

The Osages comprised the largest tribe of the southern Siouan Indians, which also included Poncas, Omahas, Quapaws, and Kansas. The Osages were often known by their band affiliations as Great and Little Osage. These tribes migrated westward from the Ohio valley before Europeans settled in America, and the Osages occupied lands in present Missouri, Kansas, and Oklahoma. Traditionally the Osages lived in large, multifamily, earth-covered lodges; they farmed as well as hunted buffalo and other animals. They were often involved in conflict with the removed Indians and white settlers. Although the Osages were not as serious a threat as Major Hitchcock intimated, they were one of the primary reasons for the establishment of a military post on the Marmaton River in 1842. General Scott, after whom the post was named, later explained that it was "a post essential to constrain the lawless Osages." The tribe was never strong again, and the remnants were all moved into present Oklahoma by 1872.

Major Hitchcock was only one of several military officers who had recommended a fort near the Missouri border in present eastern Kansas. When the Senate requested information from the secretary of war about a post in the vicinity recommended by Hitchcock, it was reported as under study and necessary. On February 10, 1842, the garrison at Fort Wayne was ordered to abandon that post and erect a new one at a site between it and Fort Leavenworth.

The following month General Taylor appointed Captain Benjamin D. Moore, First Dragoons, and Dr. J. R. Motte, army surgeon, to select a site for the new post. Accompanied by an escort of dragoons, led by Sergeant John Hamilton, they left Fort Wayne on April 1, 1842. They found the site at the Spring River crossing of the military road, which was on

Cherokee neutral lands occupied by Cherokees. Captain Moore reported that occupied land would require purchase, which authority he did not have, and his party searched farther north. On April 8 or 9 the party, accompanied by Missouri residents George Douglass and Abraham Redfield, arrived at the Marmaton crossing of the Fort Leavenworth–Fort Gibson military road and selected the location nearby for what became Camp Scott, later named Fort Scott. Moore and Motte returned to Fort Wayne, and Sergeant Hamilton and a party of dragoons were left to begin construction of temporary quarters.

On April 22 Colonel Kearny and five companies of First Dragoons reached the site of Camp Scott on their march from Fort Leavenworth to Fort Gibson. A large force was being assembled there under General Taylor because of "the unsettled state of our relations with Mexico." Kearny, assuming that the services of the men left at the Marmaton might be required too, ordered Hamilton and his men to accompany his command to Fort Wayne, leaving the construction projects and gardens unattended.

Meantime Adjutant General Roger Jones informed General Taylor that further consideration should be given to the location of the new post at Spring River. On May 10 Taylor directed Moore to visit the Cherokees at that site and see if it could be purchased for one thousand dollars. The desired land was occupied by John Rogers (also spelled Rodgers). Moore and Dr. Josiah Simpson, army surgeon, made the offer which, according to Moore, "he declined accepting saying he would not take three times that amount if he had made no improvement on the place." No other satisfactory site could be found along Spring River, and Moore concluded the new post should be built at the Marmaton as originally planned.

The site of Fort Scott, in present Bourbon County, Kansas, is located within the Osage Cuestas. Cuestas are hills or ridges with a steep face on one side and a gentle slope on the other. The fort was built on one of those ridges, overlooking the confluence of Mill Creek with the Marmaton River.

The natural vegetation in the area was a combination of tall grass prairie and oak-hickory forest, an area of prairie (including bluestem, sideoats grama, Indiangrass, and switchgrass) interspersed with forest (including ash, elm, black walnut, hickory, cottonwood, hackberry, sycamore, maple, and several types of oak trees). Native fauna included deer, wildcat, timber wolf, gray and red fox, raccoon, opossum, squirrel, beaver, otter, muskrat, rabbit, coyote, antelope, badger, and bison (commonly called buffalo). Birds present included turkey, prairie chicken, grouse, quail, and a variety of songbirds. Fish were available in the Marmaton.

The climate is characterized by hot summers and moderate winters. The average annual precipitation is about forty inches, most occurring during the spring and summer months. January is the coldest month with an average daily temperature of 33.2 degrees Fahrenheit, and July is the hottest month with an average daily temperature of 81.2 degrees Fahrenheit. The average growing season (frost-free period) is about 190 days. Because of favorable conditions, the post gardens at Fort Scott were unusually productive, especially when compared with those at most frontier forts. When Colonel Croghan inspected the post in July 1844, he observed that "the post gardens being good, the fare is equal to every wish of the soldier." All in all it was a pleasant environment for a military installation or a city, although environment was probably not a major consideration in the selection of the site. Proximity to the Osages, the Missouri border, and the Fort Leavenworth–Fort Gibson road (supply route) were most likely the determining factors. The presence of army surgeon Motte on the site-selection commission was probably to assist in finding a location conducive to good health and sanitation.

On May 26, 1842, Fort Wayne was abandoned, and its garrison of Companies A and C, First Dragoons, under command of Captain Moore, began the march to Fort Scott. They arrived there May 30, 1842, the official date for the founding of the post. In October, Company D, Fourth Infantry, was added to the garrison, and Brevet Major William M. Graham of that company assumed command of Fort Scott. The primary duties of the garrison, in addition to construction of the post, were to keep peace between whites and Indians, particularly the Osages, patrol the western border of Missouri, provide a point of safety along the military road, and control illegal liquor trade with the Indians. In addition the dragoons often participated in exploratory expeditions of unmapped territory and assisted with the protection of traders and travelers on the western trails.

2

Building Fort Scott

The major task at Fort Scott was the construction of necessary buildings to house men, animals, and supplies. The major accomplishment of the troops stationed there was the completion, over the years, of a fine set of buildings. This fort, like most others in the West, was not a true fortification but simply a settlement. Structures were erected on four sides of the 350-foot-square parade ground. There was no wall around the post, and no defensive structure, such as a blockhouse, was constructed before the Civil War. The post was simply a base for troops and supplies, more like a small village than a fort. After the fort was abandoned, most of the buildings became the nucleus for the development of a town, a conversion accomplished with few if any changes.

According to Sergeant Hamilton, who was in charge of construction of temporary log quarters prior to the movement of troops from Fort Wayne, writing some thirty years later, he and some twenty soldiers "had finished the Commanding Officers qrs, Hospital, Qr Mrs and Com Store Houses, and other Buildings and had gardens [sic] stuff planted" when the garrison arrived. Since, as noted above, Hamilton and his men were taken back to Fort Wayne on April 22 by Colonel Kearny, his claim would appear to have been physically impossible. The veracity of Hamilton's statement is further challenged by a statement of the post surgeon that "from the occupation of the post until late in November [1842], the command was in tents, and every available man was engaged upon fatigue duty, being employed in the erection of temporary log

Log cabins such as this were built in 1842 as the first army housing and served as temporary quarters for officers and troops of the new post. Several were still standing when the fort was abandoned and were sold when the other buildings were auctioned off in 1855.

buildings." Those structures, described by one officer as "huts," apparently were used until permanent quarters were completed. When Hiero T. Wilson, partner of post sutler John A. Bugg, arrived at Fort Scott on September 13, 1843, he "found the officers and soldiers in one story log houses, the chinks filled in with common mud; . . . no floors."

Construction of buildings was one of the many duties of the post quartermaster. The quartermaster department was responsible for the provision of supplies needed by the army except food, which was the duty of the commissary of subsistence. Military supplies included more than clothing, equipment, fuel, furniture, and quarters. The quartermaster department provided transportation for all supplies, which included construction of roads and bridges, purchase and operation of wagons and draft animals, forage for the animals, and maintenance of all transport equipment. Quartermasters were in charge of all buildings, including design, construction, repair, and general maintenance of barracks, officers' quarters, hospitals, bakeries, stables, repair shops, storehouses, outhouses, and other public buildings. The quality of life at any military post depended largely on the skills and temperament of the post quartermaster.

The garrison at Fort Scott was fortunate to have the services of one of the most conscientious post quartermasters in the service during the

1840s, Captain Thomas Swords, First Dragoons, who was stationed at the post, except for short periods of leave, from July 21, 1842, until June 1, 1846. During that time the plans for all buildings at the post were arranged and most of the structures were either completed or under construction before his departure. More than any other person, Captain Swords left his mark on Fort Scott. On November 26, 1842, he wrote to his friend Lieutenant Abraham Robinson Johnston, First Dragoons, regarding Fort Scott: "we are going to make it the crack post of the frontier." It was a worthy objective, indicative of the pride Swords had in his abilities, and although Fort Scott was not the largest or most important frontier post, eventually it had a sturdy complex of handsome and comfortable facilities superior to most western forts of the era.

Although Swords assumed his duties at Fort Scott with enthusiasm, he was soon aware of the difficulties of his task. To Lieutenant Johnston he wrote: "wish you were here to consult with about matters and things, am thrown entirely upon my own resources for plans &c. Not one of them here can draw a straight line, even with the assistance of a ruler — you may judge of their qualifications in this respect." Sergeant Hamilton, who had supervised construction of the temporary quarters, was the quartermaster sergeant. It is presumed that he was in charge of soldiers detailed to work on construction projects. Skilled workers were few in number. Upon his arrival at the post in July 1842, Swords noted "there are but 3 carpenters and 2 brick layers in this comd." Because the soldiers had other duties to perform the availability of any type of workers was a serious problem in the building of Fort Scott. Funds to hire civilian workers were always limited and sometimes not available.

The shortage of labor was only one of the problems Swords faced that delayed construction of permanent quarters. Good timber was available in the area, but the dam and water-powered sawmill, which troops built on Mill Creek under Swords's direction approximately one and one-half miles west of the fort to saw lumber, was plagued with three problems: insufficient water flow during much of the year, mechanical breakdowns when water was available, and lack of skilled men to do the work. The mill had the capacity "to cut from 5,000 to 6,000 feet of plank per day," according to Swords, but it seldom if ever reached capacity. Other problems contributed to the shortage of lumber available to complete the post. In 1846 a fire in the kiln destroyed some six thousand feet of oak plank intended for flooring. In 1849 a flood on the creek carried downstream approximately twelve thousand feet of lumber, only a portion of which was recovered. Thus, while Swords had expected soon after his

Thomas Swords was born in New York City, November 1, 1806, and attended the U.S. Military Academy, 1825–1829. He joined the Fourth Infantry as a second lieutenant in 1829 and served in Alabama and Florida before his appointment as first lieutenant of dragoons in 1833. He joined the quartermaster department in 1834 and was promoted to captain in 1837. He brought considerable experience to Fort Scott, where he oversaw the construction of the post, 1842–1846. Swords married Charlotte Cotheal in 1838, and she joined him at Fort Scott in 1843. They resided, with their slaves, in one of the officers' quarters. Swords was promoted to major in 1846 and served as quartermaster for Kearny's Army of the West. He was credited with raising the first United States flag over Santa Fe. He participated in the Battle of San Pasqual, California, December 6, 1846. After Kearny's force reached San Diego in January 1847, Swords sailed to the Sandwich Islands (Hawaii) and obtained clothing and supplies for the soldiers. While returning from California with Kearny in July 1847, Swords supervised the burial of the remains of the Donner Party, which suffered a tragic loss of life while attempting to cross the Sierra Nevadas during the previous winter. Swords served with General Scott's command in Mexico in 1848 and was named brevet lieutenant colonel for meritorious conduct the same year. After the war he served in Washington, D.C., St. Louis, New Mexico, and New York City. He was promoted to lieutenant colonel in 1856 and was chief quartermaster of the military Department of the Pacific, 1857–1861. He was promoted to colonel and assistant quartermaster general in 1861. During the Civil War he was chief quartermaster of the Departments of the Cumberland and Ohio, was engaged in the Battle of Chickamauga, and was brevetted brigadier and major general. After the war he was chief quartermaster of the Department of Tennessee, 1866–1867, and the Cumberland, 1867–1869. He retired from active service on February 22, 1869, and died at New York City on March 20, 1886.

arrival at Fort Scott to complete the construction of the post by the autumn of 1843, he left there in 1846 with several buildings still under construction and some neither begun nor destined to be built. The temporary "huts" apparently were still in use. By the time Fort Scott was completed, it had served its purposes and was soon abandoned.

The plans for "the crack post of the frontier," laid down by Swords in 1842 and followed closely throughout the era of construction, had buildings arranged on four sides of a square parade ground which had its corners rather than sides at the cardinal points. The officers' quarters were on the northeast side. The northwest and southeast sides were designated for dragoon barracks and stables. The southwest side was for an infantry barracks, post hospital, and guardhouse. A storehouse for commissary and quartermaster departments was set at the east corner, and a multipurpose building at the north corner would serve as post commander's office, post adjutant's office, court-martial room, ordnance storeroom, and gun house. A brick powder magazine, flagstaff, and well canopy were to be located on the parade ground.

Swords's plans were for all structures "to be framed and weather boarded" with quarters and hospital "to consist of a basement and principal story." The "basement" of each building was at ground level, and the "principal story" was actually upstairs. The hospital had interior stairs and a piazza or porch on all four sides of the principal story. All quarters had interior and exterior stairways, giving the post a unique appearance. The officers' quarters had a third story above the principal story to provide additional living space for officers and their families. According to his plans, "the buildings are all to be furnished in a plain and substantial manner, but at the same time as much neatness of appearance to be presented as is consistent with a proper economy."

It is difficult from available records to determine exactly when each building was completed for occupancy; some were occupied prior to completion. Periodic reports on the status of construction present a time-lapse view of the building of Fort Scott. When Captain Swords sent his report "of the new works now in progress at this post" to Quartermaster General T. S. Jesup, October 1, 1843, he had been at the post almost fifteen months. Despite problems with the sawmill and the shortage of skilled laborers, much had been accomplished.

Of the five planned officers' quarters, four of which were duplexes and one a single dwelling for the post commander, one duplex was completed except for some flooring and the foundations were ready for

Sketch of soldiers' barracks, 1843, one of three erected at Fort Scott. This sketch incorrectly shows a porch on the back of the building. It does illustrate the two-story construction with an exterior stairway. The lower floor, "basement," contained kitchen, mess, storeroom, and quarters for laundresses. The upper floor, "principal story," contained squad rooms and sergeants' quarters.

Unfortunately good photographs of the original soldiers' barracks are not available. This view of one of the reconstructed barracks illustrates what the original buildings were like at Fort Scott.

Reconstructed hospital building.

two additional duplexes. Of the three barracks planned, one was occupied, the second was framed and the chimneys were up, and the third had framing ready for raising and the stonework for the chimneys was ready to be put up. Each of the barracks was designed to house approximately fifty men but could hold sixty or seventy if necessary.

One of two planned dragoon stables (as it turned out the only one built) was "covered and nearly weatherboarded in." It had room for eighty horses and was placed in use during November 1843, although the plank flooring was to wait until the other buildings were completed. The hospital, forty-eight by fifty-two feet, was completed except for flooring the upper rooms and the piazza or porch that surrounded the entire structure at the level of the upper story. It was occupied in October 1843. The storehouse for subsistence and quartermaster departments, approximately thirty-two by fifty-eight feet with a basement and loft, was completed in June 1843. The powder magazine was "nearly completed." A well sixty-five feet deep was dug on the parade ground, all but the top five feet "having been blasted through successive" layers of bedrock. Total expenditures, including the sawmill ($2,609.19), amounted to $14,630.73, and it was estimated that an additional $11,200 would be required to finish the construction plans.

Swords was disappointed that the entire complex was not completed on the schedule he had set a year earlier. He explained the reasons to Jesup:

> I regret to state that, in consequence of the absence of a portion of the Dragoons during the summer, and the want of an adequate supply of lumber, owing to the scarcity of water in the mill stream, we have not been able to finish some of the buildings commenced, and that I am not, therefore, enabled to make a more favorable report of the progress, but should we soon have a supply of water we will be able to get the three companies into the tolerably comfortable quarters by the end of the year.

Despite such good intentions, the other two barracks were not ready for occupancy until the following summer.

When Colonel Croghan made his official visit to the post in July 1844, he reported that one of the barracks would be occupied the same month and the other "before the middle of August perhaps." It was ready on September 3. Croghan praised the quality of quarters at Fort Scott, but he was critical of the overall plan. The complete enclosure of the parade ground left no room for expansion should that become necessary; the stables should have been located away from the parade ground; and the hospital should have been located away from other quarters "in some retired & quiet spot." He concluded that "the beauties and advantages of the location have been greatly marred . . . the hospital and other buildings on that face, not only shut out of view the most magnificent prairie of the country, but interrupt in the most offensive way, almost the only refreshing summer breezes."

Croghan did not mention that 1844 was an unusually wet year; in fact the largest floods in recorded history occurred in the region. The rains were good news for Swords, who declared "we now have abundance of water." Unfortunately the shaft of the sawmill was broken in March, and "the progress of the work has been in consequence very much retarded." A new shaft was made at St. Louis, shipped to Fort Scott, and installed. It was "defective" and "gave way after running 3 or 4 days." A second shaft was ordered, and on May 2 Swords reported "the Mill in successful operation." That was just in time for the high water; Fort Scott received 27.43 inches of precipitation in May and June.

Colonel George Croghan, 1791–1849, was appointed inspector general in 1825. He made one official visit to Fort Scott, in July 1844, where he found conditions above average in comparison with other frontier military posts.

It may be assumed that the mill took advantage of the high waters, although it reportedly "got somewhat out of gear from the frequent and extreme freshets." Swords expressed concern in July that if he had to discharge the civilian millwright in the move to reduce expenditures by having all work done by soldiers, "his discharge would have the effect to render the Saw Mill utterly useless to this Post." He reinforced this point with recent problems: "We have already experienced the effect of not having a competent Millwright in charge of the Saw Mill, two shafts having been broken." Despite his plea, the millwright was discharged along with all other civilian workers. The mill was closed down for almost a year.

The periodic discharge of all temporary civilian workers, as ordered by the quartermaster general to save money, created chronic labor shortages and serious construction delays at Fort Scott. Specialized craftsmen not available from the enlisted ranks were engaged from distant places such as St. Louis and could not be replaced easily.

The floods in 1844 did much damage to the road between Fort Scott and Fort Leavenworth, washing out several bridges. This affected the supply route to Fort Scott, and repairs took manpower away from the garrison. In August 1844 Brevet Second Lieutenant Edmunds B. Holloway, Company C, Fourth Infantry, was reported as absent from Fort Scott "with a Detachment repairing Military road leading to Fort Leavenworth."

By 1844 Swords was able to draw upon some skilled soldiers to help with construction. In July he reported twelve craftsmen available for extra duty but declared there were no stonecutters, bricklayers, nor plasterers, without whom the fireplaces could not be constructed nor the walls plas-

Officers' row, 1873.

Officers' row at Fort Scott prior to 1900. The buildings were sold in 1855 and used in the town of Fort Scott for many years. This view shows all four buildings with only slight exterior remodeling. That these buildings were used partially accounts for their preservation.

Restored officers' quarters.

tered. The absence of dragoons in the field during summer months reduced the number of soldiers available for extra duty. As Swords stated in August 1844, "the Dragoons having been again withdrawn from the Post, and our working force in consequence much reduced but very little progress has been made in the buildings during the Past-Month."

By this time Swords and the post commander, Brevet Major Graham, were aware of the realities that precluded an early completion of the post. As Graham explained in September 1844, it would take at least two more years for the sawmill to cut sufficient lumber for the task. Labor was scarce since all citizen employees had been discharged. He estimated that with good luck the buildings might be "completed during or by the winter of 1846 & 1847, but not I think before."

At the time of his writing the status of construction was: one officers' duplex occupied, one duplex scheduled for occupancy before Christmas, three barracks occupied but flooring unfinished, hospital occupied but flooring unfinished on main story and porches, dragoon stable occupied without plank flooring, and one storehouse occupied. Since there were permanent quarters for only two officers and their families, the other five officers must have been living in the temporary shelters erected in 1842. Ironically, by the time the rest of the officers' quarters were finished the garrison had been so reduced in size that the quarters outnumbered the officers.

Reconstructed dragoon stables.

Restored quartermaster and commissary storehouse.

By 1845 national attention was shifting from the defense of the Indian frontier to problems in the Southwest. Following the annexation of Texas, U.S. troops were sent there to help settle the "boundary dispute" with Mexico. Conflict in the disputed area led to war in 1846. Less attention and fewer funds were given to frontier posts such as Fort Scott, and the garrisons were reduced in size as troops were shifted to the Southwest.

Thus when Swords announced in May 1845 that the "unusually dry season" prevented the operation of the sawmill and requested funds to purchase a steam engine to power it, the request was not granted. Fewer troops also meant fewer workers.

Swords's annual report on construction, October 1, 1845, showed only a few changes from the previous year. Two sets of officers' quarters were occupied, a third set was expected to be completed before Christmas, the frame of the commanding officer's quarters was cut and ready to erect, and the frame for a building to house the post commander's office, ordnance storeroom, and gun house was up, and the magazine was finished. The flooring in the barracks and hospital had not been completed. During the previous year construction expenditures totaled $5,492.99, and Swords estimated an additional $4,500 would be "required to complete the works."

Soon after war was declared against Mexico in May of 1846, Captain Swords was transferred on June 1 and joined General Kearny's Army of the West as quartermaster. He must have welcomed the new assignment for the opportunities it presented and for the escape from the frustrations of bringing his construction plans to fruition. Considering the many obstacles he faced, his accomplishments at Fort Scott were many. His plan of the post was practical, and the buildings erected under his direction were spacious, attractive, and sound. Post Surgeon Joseph Barnes declared in 1852 that the quarters "are exceedingly roomy, well ventilated and comfortable, and with the necessary out-houses, are furnished with good drainage, preventing all accumulations of water and filth; the arrangement of the post being such, that any inattention to police would at once become apparent." When compared with most other frontier forts, Fort Scott was, thanks largely to the abilities and determination of Captain Swords, "the crack post of the frontier."

The garrison at Fort Scott was reduced to a small force of infantry during the two years of war with Mexico, averaging fewer than fifty men per month. For these troops, more than sufficient construction was completed. The new post quartermaster, First Lieutenant George W. Wallace, Company B, First Infantry, continued work on the buildings under construction as lumber, labor, and funds were available. Soon after the war concluded, Quartermaster General Jesup requested information on the status of construction and estimated costs for erection of commanding officer's quarters. Lieutenant Wallace submitted a plan of the post showing the arrangement and status of buildings.

This plan, reproduced on the following pages, showed what had been accomplished since Swords departed. By 1848 the post comprised three officers' duplexes completed, one duplex ready for plastering, three barracks completed except for some flooring, hospital, guardhouse (built of

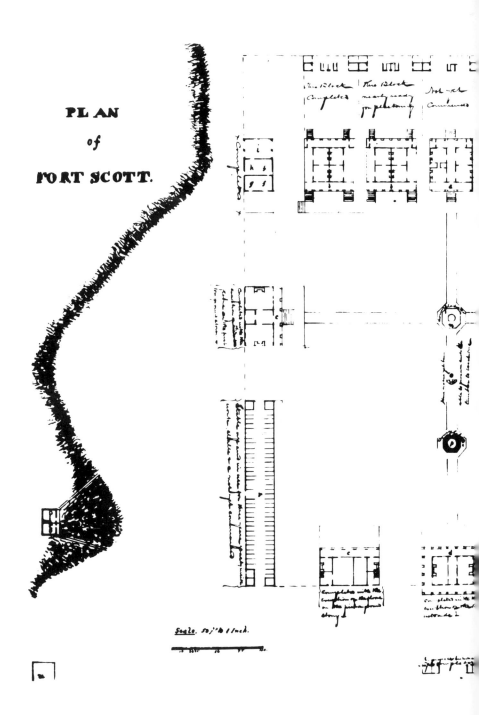

PLAN
of
FORT SCOTT.

Scale. 50' to 1 inch.

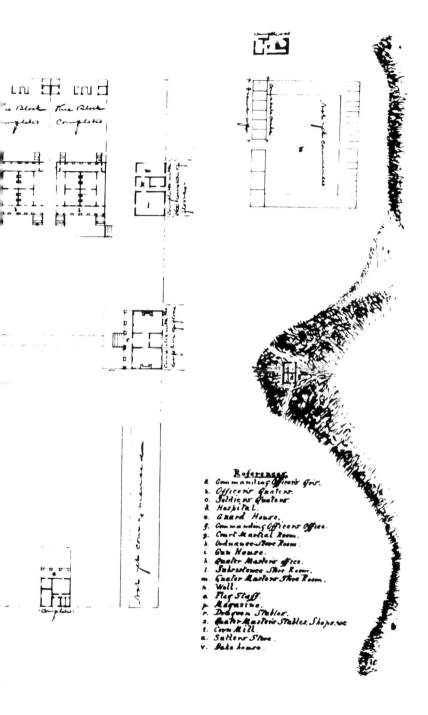

References.

a. Commanding Officer's Qrs.
b. Officers Quaters.
o. Soldiers Quaters.
d. Hospital.
e. Guard House.
f. Commanding Officers Office.
g. Court Martial Room.
h. Ordnance Store Room.
i. Gun House.
k. Qualer Masters office.
l. Subristence Store Room.
m. Quater Masters Store Room.
n. Well.
o. Flag Staff.
p. Magazine.
r. Dragoon Stables.
s. Quater Masters Stables, Shops.xc.
t. Corn Mill.
u. Sutlers Store.
v. Bake house.

31

Reconstructed guardhouse. The original building, constructed of stone, was completed by 1848. Sold along with the other buildings in 1855, it was leased back by the government during the Civil War when it was used as a hospital annex. It later became the property of the City of Fort Scott and was used as the city jail in 1900. The original was torn down in 1906.

GOV. OLD GUARD HOUSE
FORT SCOTT, KS.

Guardhouse in use as a city jail.

Reconstructed powder magazine on the parade ground.

Reconstructed well canopy on the parade ground.

Restored bake house. The bakery was completed by 1848 and supplied an important part of the daily ration for troops stationed at the post.

stone), storehouse, powder magazine, one set of stables, bake house, well with canopy, numerous outhouses, and one building containing the post commander's office, ordnance storeroom, and gun house. There is evidence of a flagstaff as early as 1844, but its size and location remain unknown. The plan included several projects under way or "not yet commenced": flagstaff at center of parade ground, commanding officer's quarters, quartermaster stable across the parade ground from the dragoon stable, and the quartermaster quadrangle, which included a corral and various repair shops east of the storehouse. How many of those projects were completed is not known, although it is certain that the commanding officer's quarters and the quartermaster stable were not built. There is evidence that a new flagstaff and the quartermaster quadrangle were completed, but at what date cannot be determined.

Brevet Captain Alexander Morrow, Company H, Sixth Infantry, became post quartermaster in the autumn of 1848. In February 1849 he requested permission to build a barn to store hay and a stable to shelter oxen. Temporary sheds to protect oxen were authorized, labor to be provided by troops. It is probable that the flagstaff, repair shops, and quartermaster quadrangle were completed under Morrow's tenure.

Morrow reported to Jesup, April 6, 1850: "According to the original plan, this Post is about finished except the Commanding officer's Quarters & another Dragoon Stable, neither of which will be wanted unless the force of this garrison is increased." The decision, dated April 25, 1850, was that no more construction was to be undertaken at Fort Scott: "The appropriation being exhausted the expenses must be reduced as much as possible." Thus, after almost eight years and expenditures of approximately thirty-five thousand dollars, the building of Fort Scott was finished. The purposes for which the frontier post had been founded were also completed. It was not a unique situation that, by the time the post was built, Fort Scott was obsolete. It was occupied until 1853 when a new post farther west, which became Fort Riley, was established. The military importance of Fort Scott, which may have been secondary to the building of the post, is a more elusive topic than the construction.

3

Frontier Defense

Although it appeared that the garrison spent much time constructing the post, Fort Scott was established to help protect the frontier. Few Indian difficulties occurred in the region after the fort was founded, and because of the absence of military demands in 1842, they were able to devote most of their time to the erection of temporary quarters and complete them before winter arrived.

On a few occasions during the 1840s troops were sent to deal with problems of Indian–white relations. On October 31, 1842, Lieutenant John Love, First Dragoons, led a small detachment to Clear Creek, Missouri, "to remove Indians." Another party of Indians was escorted from Missouri back to the reservation in 1844. On the other side troops were sent to investigate and remove squatters who were living illegally on Indian lands. On September 5, 1844, Lieutenant R. E. Cochrane, Fourth Infantry, and four infantrymen were sent to remove John Mathews from a house he was occupying on the Osage reservation. Illicit liquor traders were removed periodically from the reservations, but the flow of whiskey to the Indians was not stopped. None of those problems was serious nor threatening to the peace. At times troops accompanied missionaries to the reservations, probably more as guides than as protectors. No record was found that Indians attacked Fort Scott or even that any battles with Indians were fought near the post. Historian Henry P. Beers summed up the military realities of Fort Scott when he stated, "for military and civilian travellers on the military road Fort Scott was a way station."

This artist's concept of the completed Fort Scott depicts a courier approaching the post. Most of the fort's structures are visible in this painting. Left to right: end of the dragoon stables, company barracks, post hospital, officers' row in background, guardhouse, more of officers' row in background, another company barracks behind which is a small portion of the commissary and quartermaster storehouse, and the quartermaster repair shops and quadrangle. Painting by Gary Hawk.

One of the ironic factors in the history of Fort Scott is that the real need for a military presence in the area occurred after the post was abandoned in 1853. The border troubles in the struggle for Kansas statehood brought an era of violence that led directly into the Civil War. It was then that military action became important at Fort Scott. During the years it was active as a frontier post, 1842–1853, almost all military action occurred far from the fort. Dragoons stationed there joined in several expeditions between 1843 and 1845, but it would have been just as easy for them to participate had they been stationed at Fort Leavenworth or some other post in the region.

During the late spring and early summer of 1843, Captain Burdett A. Terrett, Company A, First Dragoons, with twenty-three men of his company, participated in an expedition to protect traders on the Santa Fe Trail. They left Fort Scott on May 26 and joined the main force of

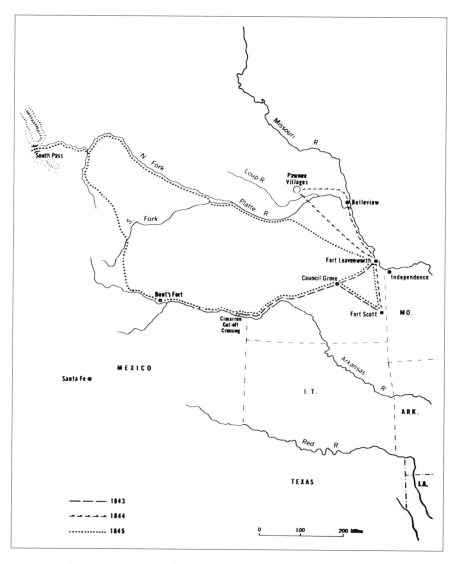

Dragoon marches from Fort Scott and Fort Leavenworth.

Dragoons in the field. Drawings by Lou Michaels.

approximately 160 dragoons from Fort Leavenworth, led by Captain Philip St. George Cooke, at Council Grove on June 4. They were to accompany the large trade caravan transporting commodities to the Southwest and provide protection from raiders reported to be coming from the Republic of Texas to attack Mexican merchants traveling the route to New Mexico.

The reports were true, and approximately one hundred Texans, led by Jacob Snively, were captured on June 30 near present Dodge City. They were disarmed by Company A, and Captain Cooke described the surrender of weapons as follows: "I directed Capt. Terrett to advance with his company — sabres drawn — and receive the arms (sending some rear rank men of the 2nd squadron afoot to put them into a wagon)."

Snively's command was then divided and those wishing to return to Texas were allowed to do so. The balance of the raiders was escorted east toward Missouri for a few days by Captain Terrett and sixty dragoons, while Cooke accompanied the traders to the international boundary at the crossing of the Arkansas River. Cooke and Terrett rejoined on July 8, and they were reportedly plagued by Texans as they marched eastward. They

were at Council Grove on July 15, and on July 20, a little east of Elm Grove, Captain Terrett and his dragoons left the main force to march to Fort Scott, where they arrived a few days later. It may be presumed that duty in the field was a welcome break from the monotony of garrison life and construction work.

As a result of the Cooke–Snively confrontation, the Republic of Texas submitted formal protests to the U.S. government. A court of inquiry was convened to investigate the military action, and Cooke was exonerated of any improper action.

Fearing that Texans might retaliate with additional raiding parties along the Santa Fe Trail, General Edmund P. Gaines, commanding the western department, ordered another escort for the trade caravan going to Santa Fe in the late summer of 1843. Cooke again led a force from Fort Leavenworth to Council Grove, where he was joined by a platoon of dragoons from Fort Scott, commanded by Second Lieutenant Richard S. Ewell, accompanied by Second Lieutenant Allen H. Norton, Fourth Infantry. The caravan, 140 wagons owned by Mexican traders, was delayed by rains, and the dragoons traveled ahead. At the Little Arkansas

39

River, dragoons from Fort Gibson under command of Captain Enoch Steen arrived to bolster Cooke's force. These fifty-four dragoons were low on provisions, many were sick, and more than half of their horses were unfit for service. Cooke selected twenty-five from the detachment to join his expedition and sent the others back to Fort Gibson.

There were no additional Texan raiders, but the Mexican traders wanted the escort to accompany them to Santa Fe. That became unnecessary when an escort of Mexican troops was met at the Arkansas River crossing. After seeing

Richard S. Ewell

the caravan safely across on October 4, the dragoons quickly marched to their home stations. It snowed after they passed Council Grove. On October 24 the dragoons from Forts Scott and Gibson took the military road south of Fort Leavenworth and traveled together until they reached Fort Scott on October 28 or 29; from there the Gibson troops proceeded.

During the summer of 1844 the dragoons from Fort Scott joined another expedition organized at Fort Leavenworth. Led by Major Clifton Wharton, First Dragoons, the five companies, including Company A led by Captain Terrett from Fort Scott, traveled to the Pawnee villages near the Platte and Loup Rivers in present Nebraska to attempt to reconcile conflicts between the Pawnees and Sioux and to impress the Indians of the region with the military strength of the U.S. government.

Company A marched from Fort Scott on July 5 with two officers, Terrett and Lieutenant William Eustis, three sergeants, three corporals, a bugler, a farrier and blacksmith, and forty-five privates. They remained at Fort Leavenworth until the expedition started on August 12. Lieutenant Eustis did not go with the command but returned to Fort Scott, where he arrived August 19. It may have been that his health was not up to the rigors of an extended march into Indian country; he had returned to duty at Fort Scott on May 13, 1844, from an extended sick leave of more than one year. In fact, his illness dated from January 1843. He would lead the dragoons from Fort Scott on an expedition to the Rocky Mountains in 1845.

Philip St. George Cooke   *James Henry Carleton*

Other dragoon officers making the 1844 trip included four captains, Cooke, Moore, John H. K. Burgwin, and William M. D. McKissack; six lieutenants, Philip Kearny, Andrew J. Smith, John Love, Thomas C. Hammond, George T. Mason, and James H. Carleton, who kept a "logbook" (later published with the journal he kept of the 1845 expedition as *The Prairie Logbooks*); Surgeon Samuel De Camp; Chaplain Leander Ker; and an Indian guide who proved to be of little help.

Lieutenant Carleton vividly described the dragoons and their horses as they formed into line before passing in review and departing on the expedition:

> The companies break into column, move off, and take position according to rank, in line. There are five of them — first, that is Capt. Cooke's troop of blacks, just wheeling into line on the left of the Band — second, this is Capt. Burgwin's troop of greys — third, that is Capt. Moore's troop of bays — fourth, that is Lieut. Kearney's troop of chestnuts — fifth, that is Capt. Terrett's troop of blacks; hardy, dashing looking fellows, those men, tanned up in their march from Fort Scott, from whence they have just joined us.

Wharton attempted to locate a new, direct route to the Pawnee villages, but his command became lost and had a difficult time reaching the Platte, where they arrived August 27. Several of the men became ill and two died while they were "wandering in the wilderness." Wharton did meet with leaders of four Pawnee bands, who promised to remain peaceful and adhere to the terms of treaties they had earlier signed, and visited several other tribes, including Oto, Potawatomi, Iowa, Sac, and Fox. The Sioux were not met nor impressed. The accomplishments of the expedition were questionable. The dragoons had gained some experiences in Plains travel that would be of benefit in ventures to the Rocky Mountains in 1845 and to New Mexico in 1846.

One dragoon company (K) remained at the Great Nemaha Subagency to assist with the distribution of annuities. The remainder of the command arrived back at Fort Leavenworth on September 21. Captain Terrett and his company (A) returned to Fort Scott on September 28. This company marched the following summer without Terrett's leadership. He was accidentally killed at Fort Scott in March 1845, after which Lieutenant Eustis was promoted to captain and assumed command of the company. Second Lieutenant Carleton was transferred to Company A and promoted to first lieutenant. He joined the company at Fort Leavenworth just prior to the expedition of 1845 and became part of the garrison at Fort Scott at the end of that expedition.

While the dragoons were recuperating from their summer trek, post commander Graham was notified that Indians from the reservation, perhaps Osages although not specified, were harassing settlers in Missouri. He sent Second Lieutenant Benjamin A. Berry, Company C, Fourth Infantry, with a small detachment to remove the "Indians from the State of Missouri into the Indian line" or reservation. The detachment left Fort Scott on November 28 and returned on December 9, 1844. This incident is noteworthy because it is the best documented example of the troops at Fort Scott performing the primary mission for which the post was founded.

The last expedition in which dragoons from Fort Scott participated prior to the war with Mexico was Colonel Stephen W. Kearny's South Pass Expedition to the Rocky Mountains in 1845. Ostensibly, the dragoons were to protect emigrants on the Oregon Trail, impress the Indians of the region with the military strength of the United States, protect caravans returning from New Mexico on the Santa Fe Trail, and conduct a military reconnaissance of the Oregon road as far as South Pass in present Wyoming.

There may have been other motives of national security, given the state of relations with Great Britain over the Oregon country and with Mexico over the Texas boundary. Each posed the threat of war. Should the British choose to fight rather than negotiate an Oregon settlement, Kearny and the dragoons would be near enough to occupy the area claimed by the United States. The troops may have been under orders to return along the Santa

Fe road in case of war with Mexico over the annexation of Texas. If Mexico were contemplating war, the show of force along the northern border might have a preventive effect on the authorities in Santa Fe and Mexico City.

Whatever the motives, Kearny departed from Fort Leavenworth on May 18, 1845, with a total command of 280 men, including Company A from Fort Scott. Captain Eustis and fifty-four men had left there for Fort Leavenworth on May 3. Second Lieutenant Richard S. Ewell, Company A, who had been absent from Fort Scott since May 3, 1844, on recruiting service, rejoined the company at Fort Leavenworth in time to accompany the expedition. Lieutenant Carleton, as noted, joined the company there too. At least six privates of Company A did not march from Fort Leavenworth, perhaps for reasons of health, and they returned to Fort Scott on May 22 and 23.

The five companies of dragoons (A, C, F, G, and K), according to Kearny, were "well mounted and equipped for any service; each dragoon having his proper arms — a sabre, carbine, and pistol." The troops protected travelers along the Oregon Trail to South Pass, reached on June 30, although Company A remained in camp near Fort Laramie and did not travel to the Continental Divide. After the others returned to Fort Laramie, the entire command marched south along the eastern edge of the Rocky Mountains to the Arkansas River and arrived at Bent's Fort on July 29. They followed the Santa Fe Trail back to Fort Leavenworth, completing the twenty-two-hundred-mile journey on August 24, having been gone ninety-nine days. Company A had separated near Council Grove on August 20 and marched directly to Fort Scott, arriving there on August 24. Not one man was lost from the entire command, and only one had suffered serious injury.

During the journey Kearny met with representatives of several Indian tribes, including Sioux, Cheyenne, and Kiowa, and asked them to let the wagons pass through their country without resistance or harassment. They promised not to disturb American travelers. It was the hope of military and civilian officials alike that the march of the dragoons would so impress the tribes that they would respect all travelers. Before the impact could be assessed, war was declared on Mexico, and the entire history of the nation and the West, including the Indians, was changed. The major value of the South Pass Expedition of 1845, as it turned out, was the experience of traveling far from a supply base on the Plains, experience that was invaluable to Kearny and the dragoons the following year when they were sent along the Santa Fe Trail to invade Mexican Territory and conquer New Mexico and California.

Fort Scott was affected by the war. The dragoons, who had been part of the garrison except for field duty since the post was founded, were sent

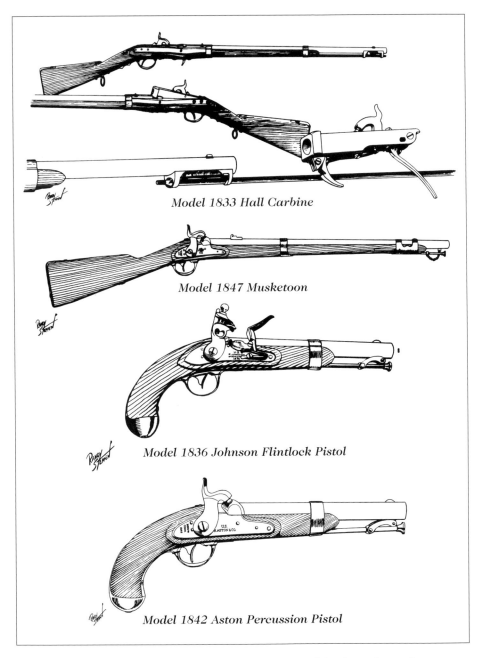

Model 1833 Hall Carbine

Model 1847 Musketoon

Model 1836 Johnson Flintlock Pistol

Model 1842 Aston Percussion Pistol

These or similar weapons, in some cases later models than shown here, were issued to dragoons or mounted riflemen who served at Fort Scott. Drawings by Randy Steffen.

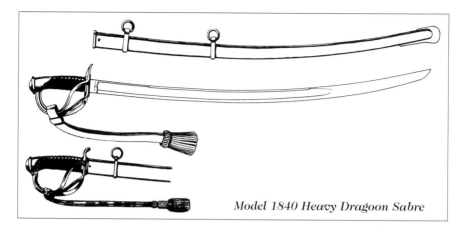

Model 1840 Heavy Dragoon Sabre

to fight in Mexico. Company A, which, in December 1845, had lost Second Lieutenant Ewell through promotion and transfer to Company G and had gained a new officer in Second Lieutenant Joseph H. Whittlesey, departed forever from Fort Scott on June 4, 1846. The men marched to Fort Gibson from where they later joined General Taylor's command in time to participate in the Battle of Buena Vista. Post quartermaster Thomas Swords, who was promoted to major on April 21, left the fort on June 1 to become quartermaster for Kearny's Army of the West, organized at Fort Leavenworth to march to Santa Fe and beyond. For the duration of the war, the fort was held by Company B, First Infantry, Captain Sidney Burbank in command. Available records suggest the troops had no other tasks than those of routine garrison duty during that time.

It should be noted that many of the former officers and men who served at Fort Scott distinguished themselves during the war with Mexico, and several were killed in that conflict. Benjamin D. Moore, founder and first commanding officer, died at San Pasqual, California, December 6, 1846. William M. Graham, Fort Scott's second commanding officer, died at Molino del Rey near Mexico City, September 8, 1847. Others who died in battle included Richard Cochrane and Charles Hoskins, Fourth Infantry. Allen Norton, Fourth Infantry, drowned on November 27, 1846, location unknown. Benjamin A. Berry died in a steamboat explosion near Corpus Christi, Texas, during the prelude to the Mexican War, September 12, 1845.

The Battle of San Pasqual was an excellent example of a small, vicious cavalry engagement that involved dragoons formerly stationed at Fort Scott and Californian lancers. During the main action, Captain Moore and a contingent of First Dragoons were engaged in fierce hand-to-hand combat. According to Surgeon J. S. Griffin, of approximately fifty dragoons who

This painting, The American Soldier, 1847, *by H. Charles McBarron, illustrates the uniforms worn during the era of the Mexican War. A mounted dragoon private is passing through a column of infantry; an infantry lieutenant is in the foreground.*

engaged the enemy, twenty-one were killed and seventeen were wounded. Each of the injured soldiers received two to ten lance wounds, and Captain Moore, who was killed, was pierced sixteen times. The Californian force of approximately one hundred men suffered light casualties, but they retired from the field of battle, allowing General Kearny to claim a victory.

The garrison at Fort Scott changed after the war. Company H, Sixth Infantry, arrived on September 29, 1848, and Company B, First Infantry, departed for Jefferson Barracks on October 3. Captain Albemarle Cady was the new post commander. Company F, First Dragoons, commanded by Brevet Major Philip R. Thompson (who had accompanied the survey of the Fort Leavenworth–Fort Gibson road in 1837 as a lieutenant) arrived on November 19. Thompson became post commander on June 6, 1849. Except for some dragoon marches in 1849 and 1850, garrison duty was all that was demanded of the troops there until the post was abandoned in 1853.

On March 21, 1849, Brevet Second Lieutenant John Buford, First Dragoons, led a detachment of approximately twenty-five troopers from Fort Scott to Fort Smith, Arkansas, from which point they joined an escort organized to protect California gold seekers, the "forty-niners," as far as Santa Fe. Buford was transferred to the Second Dragoons at Santa Fe. Lieutenant Delos B. Sackett was transferred to Company F, First Dragoons, and led the detachment back to Fort Scott in December 1849.

Dragoons from Fort Scott helped protect the Santa Fe Trail during 1850, a year that saw many travelers and the beginning of regular stagecoach and mail service on that route as well as a new military post, Fort Atkinson (1850–1854), located approximately two miles west of present Dodge City. On June 27 Lieutenant Orren Chapman, Surgeon Alfred W. Kennedy, eight noncommissioned officers, two buglers, one farrier, and forty-two privates of Company F left on an expedition "to headwaters of the Arkansas." They traveled as far as Council Grove, where they arrived July 3. They were to join Lieutenant Colonel V. Sumner's command on the Santa Fe road but instead marched back to Fort Scott. Dr. Kennedy and the troops were back at Fort Scott on July 12, and Lieutenant Chapman returned on July 16. In August the same detachment, this time with only thirty-eight privates instead of forty-two, left to join Lieutenant Colonel Sumner on the Arkansas River. Of this command, only Surgeon Kennedy returned to Fort Scott; the others marched on to New Mexico, where they were transferred. Sumner selected the site for the "new post on the Arkansas," later named Atkinson, early in September. Soldiers of the Sixth Infantry regiment were left to build that post which was occupied until 1854, one year after Fort Scott was abandoned. Surgeon Kennedy arrived back at Fort Scott on October 13.

Dragoon sergeant, left, and private in regulation dress uniforms (1833–1851). Drawing by Randy Steffen.

Mounted private, Second Dragoons, about 1842, illustrating regulation horse equipment, weapons, and fatigue dress. Drawing by Randy Steffen.

Company H, Sixth Infantry, comprised the garrison of Fort Scott until November 1, 1852, when two companies (A and K) of the Regiment of Mounted Riflemen arrived for the winter months. Major Winslow F. Sanderson of that regiment became post commander. No additional military activities originated at the post after the summer of 1850. So far as the Indian frontier was concerned, most activity was farther west. Camp Center, soon to be named Fort Riley, was occupied in May of 1853. It appeared that Fort Scott was obsolete. No one could anticipate what would happen following the creation of Kansas Territory in 1854. On April 22, 1853, Fort Scott was abandoned. The garrison marched to Fort Leavenworth. Ordnance Sergeant Michael McCann was left to guard the government buildings and property.

During its eleven years of occupation, Fort Scott was commanded by eleven officers, only three of whom served longer than one year. Only one held a field-grade commission: Major Winslow Sanderson, Regiment of Mounted Riflemen. One post quartermaster, Captain Thomas Swords, commanded the post for four months. One post surgeon, Alfred Kennedy, was in command for almost six weeks because of the illness of the only other officer at the fort. (For a complete list of commanding officers, see Appendix.)

A total of forty-two officers were stationed at Fort Scott during the eleven years, including seven surgeons (see Appendix) and one chaplain, Daniel Clarkson, who served at Fort Scott from July 26, 1850, to April 22, 1853. Two officers died while at the post. On March 17, 1845, Captain Terrett, First Dragoons, was dismounting from his horse on the parade ground. He had withdrawn his pistol from its holster, which was attached to the saddle, and somehow the reins became entangled in the lock. The pistol discharged and fatally wounded Terrett, who died within a few minutes.

Brevet Captain Alexander Morrow, Sixth Infantry, succumbed after several months on the sick list. He had been post quartermaster and post commander. He was the only officer at Fort Scott during much of the summer and early autumn of 1850 when his Company H constituted the entire garrison. Post Surgeon Kennedy was gone with the dragoons on their summer patrol, and he returned on October 13 to find Morrow too sick to command. Morrow had been ill since August. Kennedy assumed command until Captain Cady returned on November 24. Morrow's ailment was not identified, but he remained ill at the post until his death on January 7, 1851.

Fort Scott was built as a three-company post, but the number of troops stationed there varied considerably. The largest number was 202 recorded in 1843, and the smallest was twenty-six in 1847. (For a table of the monthly aggregate garrison, see Appendix.) Except during the era of the Mexican War and during 1851, when one company of infantry comprised

Second Lieutenant
Joseph H. Whittlesey
First Dragoons
1845–1846

Captain George A. McCall
Fourth Infantry
1843–1845

Second Lieutenant
Eugene A. Carr
Mounted Riflemen
1852–1853

Captain
Albemarle Cady
Sixth Infantry
1848–1852

Captain
Sidney Burbank
First Infantry
1845–1848

*Second Lieutenant
Robert E. Patterson
Sixth Infantry
1851–1853*

*Second Lieutenant
Delos B. Sackett
First Dragoons
1849–1850*

*Second Lieutenant
John Buford
First Dragoons
1848–1849*

*Second Lieutenant
David A. Russell
First Infantry
1845–1846*

*Among the forty-two officers who served at Fort Scott are those pictured here.
The photos were taken after they had served at this post, and they are shown
both older and with higher rank than when they were at Fort Scott. The rank,
regiment, and dates given refer to their service at the fort.*

the garrison, both mounted and infantry units were stationed at Fort Scott. The regiments represented there were the First, Fourth, and Sixth Infantries, First Dragoons, and Mounted Riflemen. The dragoons and riflemen were mounted troops, predecessors of the cavalry units they became in 1861. (For a list of companies with dates of service, *see* Appendix.)

The regiment of dragoons, successors to the one-year experimental mounted rangers, was the only mounted regiment in the U.S. Army when organized in 1833. When the Second Dragoons were organized in 1836, the original regiment was designated the First Dragoons. Two companies of First Dragoons founded Fort Scott, one of which remained at the post until the war with Mexico, and a third was stationed there after the Mexican War.

The Fourth Infantry was represented by two companies at Fort Scott before the Mexican War. Organized in 1815, the Fourth had seen action in the Seminole wars in Florida and assisted with the removal of the Cherokees. These infantrymen at Fort Scott provided much of the labor to construct the post. They performed good service for the nation during the Mexican War, during which several officers and men who had served at Fort Scott were killed. One company of First Infantry constituted the garrison at Fort Scott during that war. They continued to work on the buildings. Soon after the war one company of Sixth Infantry arrived to replace the company of First Infantry and remained until the post was abandoned.

The Regiment of Mounted Riflemen, organized in 1846 soon after war was declared against Mexico, became the Third Cavalry in 1861. Two companies of this regiment were stationed at Fort Scott during the last five months of its existence. Two riflemen officers commanded the post during its last days. Major Sanderson, as noted, was the only field-grade officer to command Fort Scott. Captain Michael F. Van Buren oversaw the closing down of the fort.

From all appearances, the officers and men at Fort Scott performed well the duties assigned them. The buildings constructed by their labor lasted far beyond the needs of the military and served the town of Fort Scott for many years. When Inspector General Croghan visited the post in 1844, he was favorably impressed with the work, training, appearance, and discipline of the troops. "I have been particularly pleased with the whole manner & bearing of this command," he declared. Of the two infantry companies at the post when he visited, Croghan wrote: "Both Comps are well practiced in the Infty drill, which is saying a great deal for them, as two thirds of their numbers have been constantly upon either extra or daily duty." Regarding discipline, he concluded: "The discipline of the post is good, in truth I have visited no garrison which in this respect has impressed me more favorably."

4

Life at the Fort

The life of the soldiers at Fort Scott was one of isolation, although occasional contact occurred with travelers on the military road, missionaries and traders on the Indian reservations, and settlers in nearby Missouri. There was no town in the vicinity. It would have been rare, indeed, although little evidence has been located to prove it, if there were not whiskey peddlers and prostitutes in the area, at least periodically. Beer, whiskey, wine, and a variety of items were available at the post sutler's store. In 1843 Captain Graham noted a grog shop fives miles distant in the state of Missouri that had been the cause of several courts martial of men charged with being absent without leave. For the most part social contacts were confined to the post, where officers associated with officers and enlisted men with their own kind. Sutler Wilson later recalled, "Fort Scott was a pleasant Post. The officers and families tho' few were sociable and neighborly. We had few visitors outside the Post." It should be noted that slaves were brought to Fort Scott by some of the officers. Captain Swords owned several, and post sutler Wilson owned six slaves when the post was closed in 1853. The slaves constituted a third class at the post, ranking below the officers and enlisted men.

Garrison duties were generally monotonous, and living conditions were not comfortable until the permanent quarters were completed. Officers and men alike lived initially in tents while temporary log quarters were built with their own labor. The log "huts" were in use for several years while the frame buildings were completed. During the early

53

years, the food was often of poor quality because it was sometimes transported over long distances and not carefully stored. Military supplies usually were transported to Fort Leavenworth on the Missouri River by steamboat and hauled from that point by wagon to Fort Scott. Later, as post gardens were tended with success, a supply of fresh vegetables was available in season. Foodstuffs were purchased from settlers in nearby Missouri, reducing the need for long-range transport and increasing freshness.

The soldiers had little variety in their diets. Soup, hash, stew, bread, salt pork, beef, beans, rice, and vegetables from the post garden were standard items, and salt, pepper, sugar, vinegar, tea, and coffee were included in the rations. A small amount of whiskey was part of the daily ration until 1830, and whiskey was issued to men on extra duty, such as construction of buildings, when Fort Scott was founded. Bread was a staple item; each soldier was to receive eighteen ounces per day or enough flour to make that much bread. Until the post bakery was completed at Fort Scott, it may be presumed that the bread was prepared along with the other food in the company mess. The bread was more or less edible depending on the quality of the flour and the baker's ability. All men took turns in the kitchen, regardless of previous experience or talent. It is believed that fireplaces were used for cooking at Fort Scott.

Clothing, equipment, and medical care, as well as room and board, were furnished to each soldier, and laundresses washed his clothes. There was little need for him to expend his own money, unless he wanted to buy something at the post sutler's store (such as tobacco, a toothbrush, beer, whiskey, candy, playing cards, pencil and paper, or other personal items), spend it on entertainment at a grog shop or brothel, or gamble, which was a favorite pastime. Some men even sent home a portion of their monthly pay of eight dollars to help their families.

Civilian post sutlers operated a general store on the post and provided many commodities and services to military personnel, settlers in the area, and Indians from the reservations. John A. Bugg, who apparently arrived with the first company of Fourth Infantry on October 23, 1842, was the first post sutler at Fort Scott. He was also the postmaster. In 1843 Hiero T. Wilson became Bugg's partner, and in 1849 Wilson purchased Bugg's interest and became the sole sutler until the fort was closed. He also became postmaster upon the departure of Bugg. Wilson stayed in the area and was one of the first businessmen of the town of Fort Scott.

Life at Fort Scott, as at all military posts, was organized under a rigid structure of time and work, guard duty, roll calls, inspections, and strict discipline. Orders came from the top down. The post commander was in charge, assisted by his staff, which included an adjutant, quartermaster, commissary of subsistence, medical officer, and company officers. The privates were led in their daily routine by noncommissioned officers: sergeants and corporals.

The daily schedule varied from year to year and season to season, depending in part on who was commandant, but a typical day was organized as follows: each of the commands was communicated by bugle call. Reveille sounded at daybreak, with first roll call a few minutes later. For mounted troops, stable call came immediately after reveille, forty minutes before noon, and again immediately after retreat at sunset. The men cleaned the stables and fed and watered the horses. Sick call also came before breakfast, at 7:10, and any who were ailing were sent to the post surgeon for examination and treatment, if needed. Breakfast call was sounded at 7:30 A.M.

Post sutler Hiero T. Wilson remained to become a founder and leader of the town of Fort Scott.

Fatigue call was sounded after breakfast, and the men were detailed from each company for such jobs as working on a construction site, cutting timber, hauling wood, working at the sawmill, cleaning the post, loading and unloading supplies, building a road, tending the post gardens, and numerous other duties. Those assigned guard duty, which was done on a rotating basis, were not assigned to work details. The guards assembled on the parade ground for inspection thirty minutes before the changing of the guard, received the orders of the day, and were assigned their respective sentinel posts at various sites around the post as well as at the guardhouse where prisoners were detained. If the prisoners were assigned to a work detail, guards oversaw their activities. Guards were on duty for twenty-

Post sutler's store, Fort Scott.

four hours and were usually divided into three reliefs. Each relief stood guard for two hours and was off for four hours on a rotating basis.

If troops were to receive drill instruction, which occurred only one or two days per week, they were called from fatigue to drill at 10:00 A.M. Recall from fatigue or drill was at 12:00 noon, with mess call at 12:05 P.M. Afternoon fatigue call was usually at 1:00 P.M., although drill or target practice might be called on some days from 1:00 to 2:00 P.M., after which the soldiers returned to fatigue duties.

The evening mess was scheduled at the company level and was governed by the completion of routine work or fatigue activities. The daily retreat ceremony (lowering of the flag) occurred at sunset, was preceded by the fourth roll call of the day, and could include an evening dress parade. In the army of the 1840s, the last bugle call of the day was tattoo, which required all soldiers to be at their quarters (tents or barracks) unless they were on special leave or guard duty. The fifth and final roll call was conducted immediately after the sounding of tattoo before the soldiers entered their quarters for the night. The routine on Sunday was different, except for those on guard duty, for there were no fatigue or drill calls. A weekly inspection of the troops at dress parade was at 10:00 A.M. on Sunday, after which the men were free.

Those who followed the prescribed routine, reported for duty, and performed their assignments — and this would include most of the troops — had free time for diversion and entertainment. Those who failed to perform were placed in confinement. Discipline was rigidly enforced, and those who violated the rules were punished. Soldiers were punished for breaches of military regulations, including absence without leave, sleeping while on duty, theft, intoxication, assault, desertion, and conduct prejudicial to good order, which covered a multitude of sins from insubordination to swearing.

Desertion was a common way to escape permanently from military duty, and the number who deserted was considerable during the years Fort Scott was an active post. The annual rate of desertion in the army before the Mexican War was more than 12 percent, and after that war it rose to 16 percent. It was higher yet after the Civil War. Among the reasons for desertion were inadequate pay, irregularity of and lengthy periods between paydays, harsh discipline, boresome garrison life, nonmilitary duties such as building quarters, and general dissatisfaction with military life. Bounties were paid by the army for the return of deserters, dead or alive. Deserters who were caught were given severe punishments in an attempt to discourage others.

Only a few court-martial records from Fort Scott have been found, but these give examples of the types of punishment enforced there in 1843. A private convicted of having spiritous liquor in his quarters was sentenced "to two months' confinement at hard labor in charge of the guard, and to forfeit fourteen dollars of his pay." Another private, charged with an unprovoked attack on a fellow private "by striking him a blow in the face with his clenched hand, and also striking him several blows with a piece of wood, one of which blows caused a cut on the back of his head" was found guilty and sentenced "to one month's confinement at hard labor in charge of the guard, and to forfeit fourteen dollars of his pay." A private convicted of desertion was sentenced to be whipped with rawhide, "well laid on," and to be docked six months' pay. Several convicted of being absent without leave, apparently at the grog shop in Missouri, were to forfeit six months' pay and serve a term in the guardhouse at hard labor for varying terms, from one to three months.

The farrier and blacksmith for Company A, First Dragoons, who was to accompany the expedition to protect traders on the Santa Fe Trail but refused to go and left the post without permission, stating he "would rather go in the guard-house than go on with the command," was deprived of his appointment as farrier and blacksmith, confined at hard labor in charge of the guard, and ordered to forfeit forty dollars of his pay. Although such punishments may have been a reason for desertion, those who argued in favor of such claimed they were necessary to prevent soldiers from choosing a sentence to the guardhouse instead of doing the work assigned.

Officers' lives differed greatly from those of enlisted men. Officers were better paid, had better quarters (once they were built), could have their families with them, and enjoyed more leisure time. Although Captain Swords once labeled life at Fort Scott as "dull, very dull," his letters also show that much was going on there. On December 10, 1844, he wrote to his friend Lieutenant Johnston:

Post Surgeon Joseph K. Barnes,
1851–1852

Every body here is hunting mad. hunting and dogs constitute their thoughts by day and dreams by night — Have caught two bucks, with the greyhounds, so that wolf chasing is thrown quite in the shade — there are a great many deer about and at least two hunters for every deer — the Delawares and Pottawattamies camped in every direction — I go out occasionally but being very very unsuccessful as usual, [do] not make a business of it —

Life is more than work and play, even at a frontier military post, and illnesses and injuries were a constant threat to the army. The post surgeon and his hospital were important to the health and well-being of the garrison. Some health problems, particularly respiratory illnesses and fevers, resulted from the inadequate quarters until permanent buildings were completed. There was a marked decline in fevers after the soldiers were housed in the spacious and comfortable barracks. Some diarrhea was associated with the water from the post well, although most soldiers adjusted quickly to it. Alcohol contributed to illnesses and death. Venereal diseases resulted from patronizing prostitutes. Many troopers were treated for injuries and wounds. Fort Scott was free from any epidemic, such as cholera, which affected many other military posts.

Altogether the health of the garrison was good, favorably comparable to any other location.

In 1852 post surgeon Joseph Barnes, who later served as surgeon general of the U.S. Army, summarized the medical history of Fort Scott. He identified the number of cases recorded there, categorized by symptoms, with the following results:

Symptoms	Number of Cases
Intermittent Fevers	1,709
Remittent Fevers	8
Respiratory Afflictions	331
Digestive Afflictions	287
Muscular Afflictions	133
Brain and Nervous Afflictions	77
Venereal Diseases	45
Abscesses and Ulcers, Surgical	145
Wounds and Injuries, Surgical	322
All Other Diseases	368
TOTAL	3,425

Of the seventeen deaths recorded at the post, six did not afford an opportunity for medical treatment: one drowned, one froze to death, one died of intoxication, two succumbed to gunshot wounds, and one was stabbed and beaten to death. Of the total number of cases treated, eleven terminated fatally: four of pulmonary consumption, three of pneumonia, two of meningitis, one of pleuropneumonia, and one of apoplexy. According to Dr. Barnes, most of the diseases of the brain and nervous system resulted from intemperance, and one fatal case of meningitis was attributed to that cause.

Intoxication was a serious problem throughout the army, and Fort Scott was no exception. It was, as noted previously, one of the major causes of behavior that led to punishment. It also contributed to illnesses, even death. Many officers spoke against the use of alcohol, and there was a concerted temperance effort at Fort Scott in 1845 when the extra-duty men all signed a petition rejecting their allowance of whiskey, which was apparently sent to Independence, Missouri, and sold. No other references to this temperance movement were found, and there were later indications of alcohol abuse.

Few records were found to indicate that the post surgeon treated civilians or Indians, but it would have been unusual if he did not do so on a regular basis. Reverend John J. Bax, S. J., of Osage Mission, visited Fort Scott in 1852 to "give the Catholic soldiers an opportunity to make their Easter as also to see the Doctor about the swelling at my neck." Bax was treated at Fort Scott and died there on August 5, 1852. Father John Schoenmakers, also of Osage Mission, was treated by Dr. Barnes at Fort Scott. In addition to seeing patients, the post surgeon had many other duties. He and his hospital attendants were responsible for diagnosis, treatment, and surgery when necessary, and their activities included such health-related duties as sanitation, diet, examination of recruits, and the maintenance of medical records. The surgeon administered the hospital, supervised all other medical personnel, dispensed drugs, served as coroner, and kept zoological, botanical, and meteorological records.

Hospital stewards and other attendants were assigned to duty on a rotating basis from the companies stationed at the post; thus, many were inexperienced when assigned and were rotated off duty about the time they gained essential experience. Their duties involved nursing care for the sick and wounded, preparing meals, providing proper diet, changing bandages, bathing hospital patients, and any other tasks ordered by the surgeon.

In addition to providing medical care, the army tried to give spiritual assistance to soldiers through the office of chaplain. Many frontier posts did not have a chaplain and neither did Fort Scott prior to 1850. It was common practice for visiting clergymen to hold services on occasion at posts without chaplains, and it is possible that was true at Fort Scott. A number of Indian missionaries passed the post, and some of them probably conducted services for the troops. Reverend R. S. Harris, Protestant Episcopal Church, visited Fort Scott in April 1844. Catholic Bishop John B. Miege visited Fort Scott on at least two occasions, once during the summer of 1851 and again in early August 1852, but by then the post had a resident chaplain. Reverend David Clarkson, Protestant Episcopal Church, arrived at Fort Scott on July 26, 1850, and remained until the post was abandoned. In addition to serving as religious leader, he was the schoolmaster for children at the fort. After Fort Scott was closed, he was the chaplain at Fort Riley until 1860.

Life at Fort Scott was never dangerous; no one stationed there was killed in battle. The work was rigorous during the years of construction, but after the post was built little was demanded of the garrison except general maintenance. Compared with other forts the quarters were comfortable, food was good, and Fort Scott was in a healthy location. The high quality of the buildings and soldier morale at Fort Scott indicate that the post was above average in structural accommodations and interior living conditions. However, conditions could not be construed as hygienically clean by modern standards. Typical living conditions at frontier forts of the era were indicated by a statement of the surgeon general that "it was safer for the men to face Indian warfare than life in the barracks." Colonel Croghan wrote of his inspection at Fort Gibson, July 1, 1844, that the quarters "are sadly out of repair and besides are very uncomfortable, . . . the wonder is not that the men became sick but that any lived."

By the early 1850s Fort Scott was more like a small village, which it was soon to become, rather than a frontier fort. It was also peaceful in the region, as it had been for years, but that was soon to change with the creation of Kansas Territory and the rise of border warfare. The need for troops at Fort Scott increased soon after the post was abandoned.

5

Territorial and Civil War Conflict

No military reservation was established around Fort Scott, as was typical, because the land had been set aside for the New York Indians. Thus, when the fort was abandoned, the buildings belonged to the army but the land did not. Only a few of the New York tribesmen ventured west to claim their land. The Treaty of 1838 by which the Indians were granted this land provided that if the Indians did not move to and claim the land within a specified period of time, the grant would be forfeited. Kansas Territory was created on May 30, 1854, opening the way for white settlement of the region. Until the status of the Indian land was determined, settlers could establish claims to the land, but they could not receive title. In 1860 a board of commissioners surveyed the New York Indian land and set aside 10,240 acres for the thirty-two valid Indian claims. The rest of the more than one million acres of the reservation was forfeited and passed to the U.S. Land Office. At this point the claims established by settlers could be honored and title granted upon payment for the land.

When the troops departed in 1853, Sergeant McCann was not the only resident of the abandoned post. Sutler Wilson, whose appointment there was to last into February 1855, remained. He wrote Secretary of War Jefferson Davis, May 22, 1854, requesting permission to remain there to trade with "Whites and Indians." "I have my Family with me, buildings built at my own expence, I have Six Servants [slaves]." Whether he received a reply from Davis is not known, but Quartermaster General Jesup, on June 21, 1854, gave Wilson permission to stay. Wilson later purchased some of the post buildings when they were sold. Former Sergeant John Hamilton returned to Fort Scott in 1853 and offered his services "to take charge of the Public buildings" for twenty-five dollars per month should Sergeant McCann be transferred. That did not happen, but Hamilton was there in 1855 to purchase some of the military property.

Settlers began arriving in the area soon after the territory was established, and some settled near Fort Scott. Wilson became alarmed and sent a warning to Jesup: "For your information there are persons coming into the territory & making settlements probably two [sic] near the Post." In January 1855 Judge Rush Elmore and District Attorney Andrew J. Isaacs requested permission to occupy some of the buildings at Fort Scott. This apparently was granted. There was a problem, however, for Sergeant McCann had permitted Thomas B. Arnett to occupy some of the quarters in 1854, to keep them "in good order," with the understanding that Arnett would vacate whenever requested. He refused to leave when asked to relinquish them to Isaacs and Elmore. The secretary of war ordered the buildings to be sold "without the land." Arrangements were soon made to dispose of all structures at public auction on April 16, 1855. The auction was conducted by Major Marshall S. Howe, Second Dragoons. (For a list of items sold and prices received, see Appendix.) The entire fort was sold for less than five thousand dollars. It immediately became the nucleus for the development of the town of Fort Scott.

The town was incorporated by the territorial legislature in 1855. Among the members of the first governing board were H. T. Wilson and Thomas Arnett, who had purchased one set of the former officers' quarters and opened it as a hotel. Wilson remained postmaster at Fort Scott until replaced by J. J. Farley, January 28, 1856. Because the incorporation was the work of the "bogus legislature," it was invalidated. The legal incorporation was accomplished on February 27, 1860. Wilson was president of the board of councilmen.

Many settlers had arrived before the Fort Scott Town Company was organized on June 8, 1857. The company sought title to the land from those who had established claims. It was incorporated in February 1860, and obtained title to 320 acres on September 17, 1860. An additional two hundred acres were added later. The company donated lots to those who had settled before it secured title, and additional land was donated

This 1858 sketch, "a peace convention at Fort Scott, Kansas," appears to be on the porch of the old enlisted men's barracks next to the hospital on the southwest side of the parade ground, known as the Western or proslavery Hotel. It is indicative of Fort Scott's position in the middle of the border troubles.

to religious denominations, to the county for a courthouse and jail, and to the federal government for the national cemetery. Bourbon County, named after Bourbon County, Kentucky, was organized under authority of the first territorial legislature on September 12, 1855. Fort Scott was selected as the county seat. Hiero T. Wilson was one of the county commissioners.

Fort Scott and Bourbon County, located on the Missouri border, were much caught up in the struggle between proslavery and free-state forces in Kansas Territory. It was a time known in the national press as "Bleeding Kansas," although that emotional terminology implied more violence than really existed. Election fraud was common however — Missouri "border ruffians" came across the border on election days to cast ballots in favor of proslavery candidates. Force and intimidation were used to drive free-state and proslavery settlers from the territory. Militia units were organized and violence increased.

Much of the struggle was over landholding rather than slavery, although whether Kansas became a free or a slave state would be decided by vote of the settlers. The real issue was not over slavery as such, because few slaves were in Kansas Territory, but whether Kansas, upon admission to statehood, would be counted on the side of the slave or free states in the division of the nation into two cultures in conflict. More free-state settlers came into the county in 1857.

The organization of armed mobs resulted in pleas to the territorial governor for military intervention. On December 21, 1857, two companies of the First Cavalry arrived at Fort Scott from Fort Leavenworth, Captain Samuel D. Sturgis in command. Their presence quieted the situation, but troubles renewed soon after the troops marched back to Fort Leavenworth on January 10, 1858. By 1858 a unique situation existed at Fort Scott. The former officers' quarters at the north end of officers' row was the Fort Scott Hotel, locally known as the free-state hotel. Directly across the old parade ground, the former barracks housed the Western Hotel, known as the proslavery hotel.

When lives were lost, two companies of First Cavalry returned to Fort Scott on February 26, 1858, led by Captain George T. Anderson. The town was safe but fighting continued in the countryside. Additional troops were sent to the area, but most withdrew on May 17, leaving a battery of artillery at Fort Scott. Because the situation was out of control, territorial governor James W. Denver went to Fort Scott in June with additional troops, commanded by Captain Nathaniel Lyon. According to the field returns filed from Fort Scott for June 1858, Captain Lyon's command included Companies B and D, Second Infantry, and sections A, C, and E, Third Artillery, a total of 117 officers and men. Governor Denver arranged a compromise and truce that lasted into November. Violence again raged in Fort Scott and, no federal troops being available, new territorial governor Samuel Medary authorized the organization of citizen militia units to restore order. John Hamilton, former sergeant of the First Dragoons, was appointed captain of one of the militia companies. Peace was accomplished in 1859. By this time the free-state interests were in control of Kansas, and the territory became a free state in 1861. Kansas and Fort Scott were soon caught up in the Civil War, in a sense a continuation of the Kansas troubles on a national scale.

Following the election of Abraham Lincoln in 1860, the nation was polarized into two uncompromising camps, North and South. Kansas and Missouri were on opposite sides, and border violence returned to the area. In December 1860 troops were stationed at Fort Scott until the following February 1, just three days after Kansas became the thirty-fourth state of a union about to divide in two. By that time it appeared that the area was quiet, but the secession of southern states soon led to the most destructive war in American history. The history of the Civil War in the region has been told many times and is beyond the scope of this booklet, but a brief look at what happened to Fort Scott during the war follows.

During the Civil War the town of Fort Scott was continually occupied by the Union army and became a huge military complex, especially when compared with the small fort of the "Permanent Indian Frontier." The military complex consisted of earthworks, lunettes, fortified artillery positions, a quartermaster depot, sub-district headquarters, general U.S.A. hospital and a military prison. On March 19, 1862, the U.S. Army officially reestablished Fort Scott as an active military post.

More troops were stationed at Fort Scott during the four years of civil war than had been there during the entire time it was a frontier military post. At the peak, in March 1864, more than sixteen hundred troops were stationed there. The garrison comprised regular army and volunteers from various states. Black regiments and units of American Indian Home Guards as well as white soldiers served there. Thousands of other troops passed through Fort Scott, which became a staging area for Union troops operating into Missouri, Arkansas, and Indian Territory (present Oklahoma). Fort Scott also became an important gathering point for refugees, including former slaves from Missouri and Arkansas and pro-Union residents of Indian Territory.

The two officers who commanded the post during most of the war were Major B. S. Henning, Third Wisconsin Cavalry, until April 1863, and Major Charles W. Blair, Second Kansas Cavalry, until December 1864. The quartermaster there during much of the war was Captain Merritt H. Insley. The names of those officers were honored in the naming of three defensive fortifications, called lunettes, constructed in the town of Fort Scott during the war. After the Civil War the post of Fort Scott was officially closed by the U.S. Army on October 10, 1865. All of the blockhouses, military surplus, and captured property were sold at a series of auctions conducted between June and December 1865.

Considerable raiding occurred back and forth along the Kansas–Missouri line throughout much of the war. On two occasions Confederate troops were close to Fort Scott. The town was never invaded, however, and most of the troops stationed there used the post as a base of operations in the region. Although the town of Fort Scott wanted military protection, relations between soldiers and civilians were not always peaceful. In early September 1861 Confederate General Sterling Price led a large rebel force in Missouri, not far from Fort Scott. Fearful of an attack on the town, many citizens abandoned their homes. The Union

This view of the Fort Scott hospital was taken during the Civil War and shows the piazza or porch that surrounded the building at the level of the "principal story" or upper floor. Behind the hospital, left, may be seen a portion of the powder magazine. Far left is the well canopy. One of the officers' duplexes is shown in the far background.

troops that remained behind looted some of the private property. Lieutenant Joseph H. Trego, Company D, Fifth Kansas Volunteer Cavalry, and seven of his fellow officers, "with four soldiers as servants and a contraband wench for cook," occupied the residence of a Mr. Williams. Trego wrote his wife:

> The parlor and one bedroom are richly furnished, fine paintings & engravings on the walls, spring bottom sofa, divan, chairs, etc. A good piano which [Adjt. C. B.] Zulasky is now amusing himself with. Preserves & jellies, magazines & book[s] and everything we want are here, so you see we are living high at present.

In the spring of 1862 two soldiers raped a girl, reportedly while her mother watched. A mob of angry citizens took them from the guardhouse and hanged them before they could be brought to trial.

It is important to note that, while many troops were stationed at Fort Scott, the federal government had sold all the public buildings there. It appears that some of the old fort buildings, as well as many other buildings in the town, were rented by the government. The old hospital, for example, was leased and used again for that purpose. The former guardhouse was rented as an annex for the hospital. There is no evidence that

This 1863 photograph of Market Street, town of Fort Scott, depicts several old Fort Scott buildings. At center is the post hospital. To the left of the hospital is the end of one barracks. A portion of one officers' duplex and the roof of another may be seen beyond the hospital. To the left of the officers' quarters is the building that contained the post commander's office, court-martial room, ordnance storeroom, and gun house. All buildings had been sold by the government in 1855, but the army leased the hospital and probably others during the Civil War.

any quarters for officers or men were constructed during the war, although some buildings may have been rented for that purpose. One inspection report, not dated but probably filed sometime in 1862 or 1863, declared that the total monthly rent paid for buildings and land used by the army in Fort Scott was $472.83, of which $123.83 was paid for the quartermaster department. This indicates that the remaining $349.00 may have been paid for the hospital and quarters to house troops. Most likely many troops were quartered in tents.

There was some military construction before the war ended, although the dates of completion remain unknown. A bridge was built across the Marmaton, probably in 1862, which later washed away. Another was built to replace it. Other buildings erected included a sta-

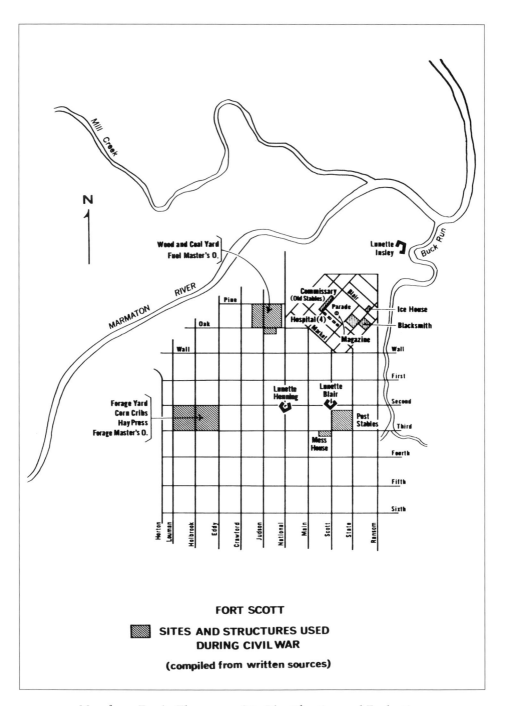

N

FORT SCOTT

SITES AND STRUCTURES USED
DURING CIVIL WAR

(compiled from written sources)

Map from Erwin Thompson, Site Identification and Evaluation.

This 1863–1865 Civil War scene depicts two men on horses in front of the stables at Fort Scott. In the foreground is Corporal George H. McCoon (company saddler), Third Wisconsin Cavalry.

ble, mess house, forage office, log prison (twenty by eighty feet, two stories high), ice house, blacksmith shop, several small storehouses, corn cribs, fences, a building for the sexton at the military cemetery, and three lunettes. One of the original national cemeteries was established at Fort Scott on November 15, 1862, on approximately ten acres of land donated in part by the city and in part by the Presbyterian congregation that had secured land for a cemetery; the remainder was purchased by the federal government at a cost of seventy-five dollars. The National Cemetery may still be visited in Fort Scott.

Three forts or lunettes were constructed in early 1863 as part of the defensive fortifications that surrounded Fort Scott. Each lunette consisted of a blockhouse, stockade, and a fortified artillery position. Lunettes Blair and Henning protected the southern approach to Fort Scott, and Lunette Insley defended the northeastern part of the town.

Lunette Blair, located near Second and Scott Streets, included a two-story log blockhouse, sixteen by sixteen feet, with shingled roof and a log palisade 369 feet long and nine feet high (six and one-half

Fort Scott National Cemetery, established November 15, 1862.

feet above ground). Apparently an earthen embankment was around the outer wall of each lunette. Lunette Insley, located northeast of the old military post, had a two-story log blockhouse, twenty by thirty feet, with shingled roof and a log palisade 326 feet long. Lunette Henning, located near Second and National Streets, had a two-story, octagon-shaped blockhouse, fourteen feet in diameter, with shingled roof and a log palisade 342 feet long.

Orders were issued to erect additional buildings, but no record of the construction was found. By order of the secretary of war, January 16, 1863, Fort Scott was declared a permanent military post. On December 1, 1864, Major General Samuel Curtis, commanding the Department of Kansas, ordered the construction of barracks and stables for one thousand men and horses. This order may have resulted in the construction of the stables and mess house mentioned previously, but apparently no barracks were built before the post was closed on October 10, 1865.

The Fort Scott Town Company filed a protest to the sale of the fort buildings, declaring that the government had not paid the rents for the land on which the structures were located. The company apparently claimed the right to the buildings in lieu of rent and damages. It was

An unidentified military band poses in front of old officers' quarters number three at Fort Scott, ca. 1861–1865.

Hospital tents on the parade ground during the Civil War. Two sets of old officers' quarters are in the background.

shown that most of the buildings were located on land owned by H. T. Wilson and J. E. Dillon. Major Theodore C. Bowles, in charge of the disposition of the buildings, noted that the rents were to be paid only until June 1, 1865, "after which they were to cease." Despite the protest, the buildings were sold. Apparently only two bidders attended the sale; perhaps they were Wilson and Dillon. Major Bowles described the bids as "very low."

With the abandonment and sale of Fort Scott in 1865, it appeared that the military history of the second oldest white settlement in Kansas was over. The Union had been preserved, and Fort Scott could look forward to growth and development along with the rest of the nation. Railroads promised a great future. The Missouri River, Fort Scott and Gulf Railroad, later known as the Kansas City, Fort Scott and Gulf Railroad, was completed to Fort Scott in December of 1869. Others followed. When the first line began to build south into the old "neutral ground" of the Cherokees, troubles arose that necessitated another military era in the history of Fort Scott.

6

The End and a New Beginning

The Missouri River, Fort Scott and Gulf Railroad (MRFS&G) planned to build all the way to the gulf, but opposition was met among the settlers of the neutral ground south of Fort Scott. The Cherokees had ceded their lands in Kansas to the federal government in 1866, with the proviso that the land would be sold at a price of not less than $1.25 per acre, mineral lands excluded, to settlers with claims under the pre-emption law. The secretary of the interior was authorized to sell all unclaimed lands in one block at a minimum price of one dollar per acre if such a contract could be negotiated. In all cases, the money paid for the land was to be deposited to the credit of the Cherokees.

In 1868 the remaining neutral lands were sold to James F. Joy, who had a financial interest in the MRFS&G. Joy later sold the lands to the railroad. Some settlers' claims were denied, ostensibly because they were on mineral (coal) lands but most likely because Joy wanted the lands for his railroad. Other settlers were told they could purchase their claims from the railroad, at a price several times greater than the government required. Because the federal government was aiding railroad expansion as essential to the economic growth of the nation, railroad interests apparently were given priority. This roused opposition among actual settlers, and a group of them formed a "land league" which was determined to stop the railroad, by force if necessary.

Remnants of Fort Scott military buildings appear in this 1950s aerial photograph. The parade ground had become a park. Old officers' row can be identified on the near side of the parade.

This 1980 aerial photograph depicts the restored Fort Scott National Historic Site, surrounded by the city of Fort Scott.

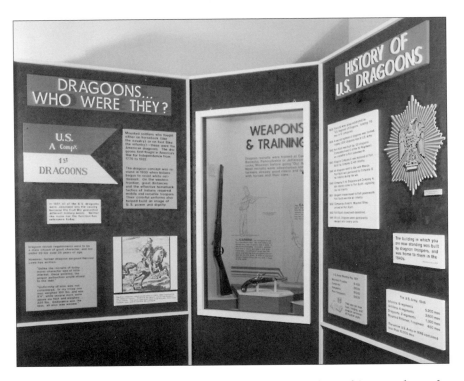

Historical exhibits in the museum at Fort Scott, such as this one about the dragoons, provide visitors with an understanding of the era and the events experienced by the soldiers stationed at the post, 1842–1853.

During the spring of 1869 railroad survey crews were harassed and construction crews were warned not to enter the neutral grounds. Some railroad property was destroyed. Violence and threats of violence led authorities to send federal troops to secure the peace. The league was not intimidated and construction crews were attacked. More troops were sent and stationed along the railroad route. Although the secretary of war reported that the presence of soldiers stopped the attacks, it was determined that they should remain in the region until railroad construction to the southern border of Kansas was completed.

On November 24, 1869, the Post of Southeast Kansas was established, with headquarters and staff at Fort Scott and with the troops stationed at four locations along the railroad route. Troops of the Sixth Infantry and Seventh Cavalry occupied the camps initially, and, later, companies of the Fifth Infantry and Sixth Cavalry performed the duties.

Restored prairie, Fort Scott National Historic Site.

In February 1870 Major James P. Roy, commanding the "troops operating in Southeast Kansas," declared:

> Until the Rail Road is completed to the state line, and through the Neutral Lands, which the Chief Engineer of the road states, will be some time in May, I am decidedly of the opinion that a portion of the troops now here should remain. It is true there has been no disturbance of any kind since the troops have been stationed here, but I ascribe this to the moral effect of their presence, as the settlers evince much hostility against Mr. Joy, the owner of the lands.

The troops were not popular with the settlers, who claimed their presence was proof that the federal government was taking the side of Joy and the railroad. As with the first Fort Scott, the presence of troops continued to maintain peace. The league, unable to stop the railroad by force, turned to the courts for relief.

The troops were called upon to assist with the protection of Indian lands from encroachment by settlers and invasion by illegal whiskey vendors. They also assisted with the final removal of the Osages from Kansas to present Oklahoma and helped protect that tribe from whites who were located there.

Infantry guard detail during a Living History Weekend at Fort Scott National Historic Site.

The land claims in the neutral ground were apparently resolved in the courts in favor of the railroad before the end of 1872. The settlers gave up their opposition. Once more, and for the last time, Fort Scott ceased to be a military post. On April 16, 1873, the Post of Southeast Kansas, headquartered at Fort Scott, was abandoned. The garrison was transferred to Fort Gibson, Indian Territory. The city of Fort Scott continued to expand, engulfing the remnants of the original military post.

Many of the old fort buildings survived in downtown Fort Scott, serving a variety of residential, business, and professional purposes over the years. Some were extensively remodeled, some were destroyed by fires, and others were torn down to make room for more modern structures. Fort Scott took pride in the military origins of the community. It was not, however, until the 1950s that a group of history-minded citizens became serious about restoring the fort to its original appearance to commemorate the heritage of the town and attract visitors to an educational museum. Much planning and hard work resulted in 1965 in congressional establishment of the Fort Scott Historical Area. This was a joint project of the City of Fort Scott and the National Park Service, with federal funds to assist the restoration. Research began that led to the development of

Parade ground, Fort Scott National Historic Site.

plans to purchase all the property that the original fort had occupied, restore what buildings remained, and reconstruct what had been destroyed to recreate the post as it had looked in the early 1850s.

Fort Scott was an ideal example of the pre-Civil War frontier military post, and the fact that nine of the original buildings had survived more than a century made the project feasible. Funds were appropriated and the work began. In 1978 Congress established Fort Scott National Historic Site, and the National Park Service replaced the City of Fort Scott as administrator in 1979. This remarkable exhibition of buildings, museum collections, and living-history activities commemorates the history of an army post on the Indian frontier, 1842–1853, with interpretive materials on the military uses of the site before, during, and after the Civil War. Here visitors of all ages can enjoy, understand, and appreciate this important heritage.

APPENDIX

COMMANDING OFFICERS OF FORT SCOTT, 1842–1853

Captain Benjamin D. Moore, First Dragoons, May 30, 1842–October 23, 1842

Brevet Major William M. Graham, Fourth Infantry, October 23, 1842–July 21, 1845

Captain Sidney Burbank, First Infantry, July 21, 1845–December 18, 1845; April 19, 1846–September 30, 1848

Captain Thomas Swords, First Dragoons, December 18, 1845–April 19, 1846

Captain Albemarle Cady, Sixth Infantry, September 30, 1848–February 6, 1849; November 24, 1850–October 6, 1852

*Brevet Captain Alexander Morrow, Sixth Infantry, February 6, 1849–June 6, 1849; April 7, 1850–October 13, 1850

Brevet Major Philip R. Thompson, First Dragoons, June 6, 1849–April 7, 1850

**Assistant Surgeon Alfred W. Kennedy, October 13–November 24, 1850

First Lieutenant Thomas Hendrickson, Sixth Infantry, October 6–November 2, 1852

Major Winslow F. Sanderson, Mounted Riflemen, November 2, 1852–January 6, 1853

Captain Michael Van Buren, Mounted Riflemen, January 6–April 22, 1853

*Morrow was relieved of command October 13, 1850, because of illness. He died at Fort Scott, January 7, 1851.

**Dr. Kennedy, the only other officer at the post, replaced the sick Morrow as commanding officer. It was one of the rare instances where a post surgeon commanded a frontier military post.

POST SURGEONS AT FORT SCOTT, 1842–1853

Josiah Simpson, May 30, 1842–December 4, 1842
Joseph Walker, November 13–24, 1842; December 4, 1842–July 20, 1847
Richard French Simpson, May 4–June 2, 1844
William Hammond, July 20, 1847–August 28, 1848
Alfred W. Kennedy, August 28, 1848–June 27, 1850; July 12–August ?, 1850; October 13, 1850–April 30, 1851
Joseph K. Barnes, April 26, 1851–September 1, 1852
Levi H. Holden, October 10, 1852–April 22, 1853

Fort Scott Aggregate Garrison Present, End of Month Report, 1842–1853
(Includes sick and prisoners; does not include those absent from post)

YEAR	JAN	FEB	MAR	APL	MAY	JUN	JLY	AUG	SEP	OCT	NOV	DEC
1842					120	123	129	125	127	177	196	190
1843	202	193	202	195	164	169	188	162	157	170	171	162
1844	155	148	142	128	157	155	102	84	152	148	137	143
1845	144	142	136	139	114	110	49	97	98	91	92	85
1846	77	80	93	95	99	46	44	42	42	39	34	42
1847	27	27	26	85	82	78	72	72	68	67	67	65
1848	63	62	61	60	60	61	34	33	80	47	104	103
1849	107	101	70	68	73	73	71	73	71	71	74	111
1850	109	110	110	109	106	53	83	54	51	56	53	42
1851	42	42	40	36	51	51	51	47	45	50	51	51
1852	48	43	49	49	40	42	43	41	41	42	152	155
1853	156	156	155	144								

Companies Stationed at Fort Scott, 1842–1853

FIRST DRAGOONS
> Company A, May 30, 1842–June 4, 1846
> Company C, May 30, 1842–May 2, 1843
> Company F, November 19, 1848–August ?, 1850

FIRST INFANTRY
> Company B, July 14, 1845–October 3, 1848

FOURTH INFANTRY
> Company C, May 3, 1843–July 21, 1845
> Company D, October 23, 1842–July 21, 1845

SIXTH INFANTRY
> Company H, September 29, 1848–April 22, 1853

MOUNTED RIFLEMEN
> Company A, November 1, 1852–April 22, 1853
> Company K, November 1, 1852–April 22, 1853

Account of Sales of Buildings and Other Public Property at Fort Scott, Kansas Territory, April 16, 1855

No.	Names	Description	Amount
1	Wm. Barbee	Log Crib, Log ox shed, & rails enclosing the same, near Saw Mill	$16.00
2	John Conner	2 log huts & rails enclosing them	5.00
3	A. Masters	1 log hut near Mill bank	2.50
4	A. Masters	Saw Mill	50.00
5	Wm. Barbee	1 log hut on hill outside of enclosure	1.50
6	H. T. Wilson	Blacksmith shop & Roothouse, near Sutler Store	25.00
7	James Kill	Stone Sink, near Sutler Store	6.00
8	James Kill	Rails enclosing 126 acre lot	65.00
9	Thomas Watkins	Hay Scale House	50.00
10	B. F. Hill	Rails enclosing small lot in front of hay scale & 2 gates one near Hay Scale House	5.50
11	John Linn	4 log huts & rails enclosing them near hay scale	19.50
12	Wm. Barbee	Log (Slaughter) hut & pump	1.00
13	John Linn	Small sheds & rails enclosing, opposite side of creek from slaughter hut	11.00
14	Robert Kill	Log hut near ox yard	2.00
15	J. M. Linn	Rails enclosing ox yard with shed enclosed	13.00
16	Wm. Barbee	Roothouse & Stone Sink, S.E. Cor. of garrison	2.00
17	John Hamilton	Rails enclosing garden & Hut, opposite side of creek, East corner of garrison	14.00
18	John Hamilton	Log hut near Bake House	6.00
19	D. F. De Wint	Small lot of rails in rear of 4th off. Qrts	4.00
20	James Kill	Bake House	70.00
21	Thomas Watkins	9 large posts	4.00

22	T. F. Whitlock	Qr. M Stable & shed, Corn Crib & shops	405.00
23	H. T. Wilson	Blacksmith Shop & Carpenter Shop (wood)	60.00
24	H. T. Wilson	loose lumber in shop	11.00
25	James Kill	Qr. Mrs. & Subsistence Store House	134.00
26	James Kill	Company quarters East corner	200.00
27	J. M. Mitchell	Guardhouse	151.00
28	H. T. Wilson	Well cover & posts	28.00
29	T. S. Dodge	Magazine	50.00
30	T. F. Whitlock	Case of drawers in hospital	20.00
31	C. T. Hayden	Copper Boiler in Hospital	5.00
32	T. F. Whitlock	Hospital	400.00
33	T. S. Dodge	Compy Quarters, West Cor	300.00
34	T. S. Dodge	Stable	200.00
35	Geo. Oldham	Compy Qrts N.W. Corner	200 00
36	Wm. Barbee	Adjts office & gun house	200.00
37	A. Hornbeck	1st block offrs quarters	350.00
38	H. T. Wilson	2d block offrs quarters	300.00
39	G. M. Stratten	3d block offrs quarters	505.00
40	C. Mitchell & T. S. Burgess	4th block offrs quarters	425.00
41	D. F. De Wint	Smoke house in rear of 4th off Qrts	10.00
42	G. M. Stratten	Smoke house in rear of 3d off Qrts	10.00
43	H. T. Wilson	Smoke house in rear of 2d off Qrts	5.00
44	H. Procter	Rails enclosing 2 small [?] in rear of Adjts office	4.50
45	James Miller	Ice house & 2 Loghouses near Ord Sergt. Qrts	5.00
46	T. Shoemaker	Hut occup by Ord Sergt & shed in enclosure, rails enclosing	60.00
47	T. Shoemaker	Rails round Ord Sergts garden	10.00
48	Geo. Oldham	12 bunks in north set of Barracks	2.50
49	T. S. Dodge	10 bunks in west set of Barracks	2.50
50	B. F. Dodge	Small Building	1.00
51	B. F. Dodge	Fence enclosing Parade Grounds	11.00

52	John Herford	Lightning rod & staff & Flag staff	1.00
53	Peter Duncan	Wardrobe in east end 4th block	9.00
54	T. S. Burgess	Sideboard in east end 4th block	13.00
55	D. F. De Wint	Wardrobe & Sideboard in North end 4th block	13.00
56	A. Masters	Wardrobe in East end 3d block	10.00
57	A. Margrave	Sideboard in East end 3d block	11.00
58	D. F. Greenwood	Sideboard & Wardrobe in Nth end 3d Block	28.00
59	H. T. Wilson	2 Wardrobes & 2 Sideboards in 2nd Block	60.00
60	A. Hornbeck	1 Wardrobe & 1 Sideboard E. end 1st Block	25.00
61	Wm. Barbee	1 Wardrobe & 1 Sideboard North end 1st Block	25.00
62	S. A. Williams	Large table in Hospital	4.00
63	H. Bloomfield	Benches in Hospital	1.50
64	Wm. Barbee	Benches in Hospital	1.50
65	S. A. Williams	Ladder	1.00
66	B. F. Hill	Bottles	1.00
67	A. Hornbeck	Tables & Benches in North Brks	3.00
68	Wm. Barbee	Tables & Benches in West Brks	4.00
69	B. F. Hill	Tables & Benches in East Brks	1.00
70	D. Bloomfield	10 Bunks in East Brks	1.00
71	T. F. Whitlock	Small lot Stair posts	5.00
72	Cash	Small table in Hosp	.50
73	Cash	2 old Sabre blades	.50
74	J. Conner	Boxes &c belonging to Co. A, 1st Drags	4.50
			$4,666.00
		Deduct 5% Auctions fee	233.30
			$4,432.70

Further Reading

Barry, Louise. *The Beginning of the West: Annals of the Kansas Gateway to the American West, 1540–1854.* Topeka: Kansas State Historical Society, 1972.

Beers, Henry Putney. "The Western Military Frontier, 1815–1846." Ph.D. diss., University of Pennsylvania, 1935.

Carleton, J. Henry. *The Prairie Logbooks: Dragoon Campaigns to the Pawnee Villages in 1844, and to the Rocky Mountains in 1845.* Edited by Louis Pelzer. Chicago: Caxton Club, 1943.

DeVoto, Bernard. *The Year of Decision, 1846.* Boston: Little, Brown and Co., 1943.

Goodlander, C. W. *Memoirs and Recollections of the Early Days of Fort Scott.* Fort Scott, Kans.: Fort Scott Monitor, 1899.

Lowe, Percival G. *Five Years a Dragoon, '49 to '54.* Norman: University of Oklahoma Press, 1965.

Monaghan, Jay. *Civil War on the Western Border, 1854–1865.* Boston: Little, Brown and Co., 1955.

Myers, Harry C., ed. *From the Crack Post of the Frontier: Letters of Thomas and Charlotte Swords.* Topeka: Kansas State Historical Society, 1983.

Oliva, Leo E. *Soldiers on the Santa Fe Trail.* Norman: University of Oklahoma Press, 1967.

Prucha, Francis Paul, ed. *Army Life on the Western Frontier: Selections from the Official Reports Made Between 1826 and 1845 by Colonel George Croghan.* Norman: University of Oklahoma Press: 1958.

Prucha, Francis Paul. *Sword of the Republic: The United States Army on the Frontier, 1783–1846.* New York: Macmillan Co., 1969.

Rickey, Don. *Forty Miles a Day on Beans and Hay: The Enlisted Soldier Fighting the Indian Wars.* Norman: University of Oklahoma Press, 1963.

Robley, T. F. *History of Bourbon County, Kansas, to the Close of 1865.* Fort Scott, Kans., Fort Scott Monitor, 1894.

Steffen, Randy. *The Horse Soldier, 1776–1943, Volume I: The Revolution, the War of 1812, the Early Frontier, 1776–1850.* Norman: University of Oklahoma Press, 1977.

Welch, G. Murlin. *Border Warfare in Southeastern Kansas, 1856–1859.* Pleasanton, Kans., Linn County Historical Society, 1977.

Acknowledgments

The author has relied heavily upon research conducted by others in the preparation of this material and wishes to express thanks particularly to the excellent work by Louise Barry, Erwin N. Thompson, Sally Johnson Ketchum, and Harry C. Myers. Present and former staff members at Fort Scott National Historic Site have given encouragement, provided information, made numerous helpful suggestions, and saved me from more than a few errors, and I thank especially Harry Myers, Sheridan Steele, Randy Kane, and Arnold Schofield. The support given by the staff at the Kansas State Historical Society, who did the hard work of editing and seeing this through press, is appreciated more than words can express. The archeological investigations at Fort Scott by Thomas Barr, written by John Reynolds, were helpful. Robert Knecht, Kansas State Historical Society, and Marc Campbell, formerly with Forsyth Library at Fort Hays State University, arranged the loan of microfilmed records of Fort Scott. My friend and former colleague in the history department at Fort Hays State University, Wilda M. Smith, came to my rescue with a microfilm reader and typewriter when my own equipment failed. Special thanks are due the Friends of Fort Scott, Limited, for permission to reproduce illustrative materials. The invaluable drawings of the late Randy Steffen are reproduced here through the generosity of Dorothy Steffen Spencer and the University of Oklahoma Press. My partner, Bonita, made it possible for me to devote the time necessary to complete this project and tolerated my preoccupation with writing when other things needed to be done. Her support deserves more than thanks.

ILLUSTRATION CREDITS

Facing title page: New York Historical Society, New York City; 2, 5, 6 Kansas State Historical Society (KSHS); 7 lithograph from Fayette Robinson, *Organization of the Army of the United States* (1848); 9 drawing from Thomas Donaldson, *The George Catlin Indian Gallery in the U.S. National Museum* (1887); 11, 12 KSHS; 18, 20 Fort Scott National Historic Site; 22 (top) drawing from T.F. Robley, *History of Bourbon County, Kansas, to the Close of 1865* (1894); 22 (bottom), 23 Fort Scott National Historic Site; 25 lithograph from Fayette Robinson, *Organization of the Army of the United States* (1848); 26 (top) KSHS, courtesy of Robert Stevens; 26 (bottom), 27, 28 Fort Scott National Historic Site; 30–31 National Archives, Washington, D.C.; 32 (top) Fort Scott National Historic Site; 32 (bottom) KSHS; 33 Fort Scott National Historic Site; 36 Historic Preservation Association of Bourbon County; 37, 38, 39 Fort Scott National Historic Site; 40, 41 (left) Department of the Army, U.S. Military History Institute; 41 (right) courtesy Museum of New Mexico, neg. #22938; 44, 45, 48 *The Horse Soldier, 1776–1943, Volume I: The Revolution, the War of 1812, the Early Frontier, 1776–1850* (1977), courtesy of Dorothy Steffen Spencer and University of Oklahoma Press; 46, 50, 51 Department of the Army, U.S. Military History Institute; 55 Historic Preservation Association of Bourbon County; 56 drawing from T.F. Robley, *History of Bourbon County, Kansas, to the Close of 1865* (1894); 58 Department of the Army, U.S. Military History Institute; 65 Culver Pictures; 68, 69 Fort Scott National Historic Site; 70 National Park Service; 71 Fort Scott National Historic Site; 72 *Fort Scott Tribune*; 73, 76, 77, 78, 79, 80, 81 Fort Scott National Historic Site.

This publication has been financed in part with federal funds from the National Park Service, a division of the United States Department of the Interior, and administered by the Kansas State Historical Society. The contents and opinions, however, do not necessarily reflect the views or policies of the United States Department of the Interior or the Kansas State Historical Society.